# WHAT PEOPLE ARE SAYING ABOUT *A FAITH THAT IS REAL*

*Read this book with an open Bible and an expectant heart!*

—FROM THE FOREWORD BY LUIS PALAU,
WORLD-RENOWNED EVANGELIST, BROADCASTER, AND AUTHOR OF *STOP PRETENDING*

*With true life experiences and insights, Dan Owens delves into the book of James with passion and care. Like the book of James itself, there is no sugar coating in these pages—it is raw, real, and relevant. We, the church, need to wake up! Dan's words encourage us to not only embrace the truth, but live it loud.*

—DAVID M. EDWARDS
WORSHIP ARTIST AND AUTHOR OF *WORSHIP 365: THE POWER OF A WORSHIPING LIFE*

*Authenticity is the Christian's strongest defense against the world's accusation of hypocrisy. Dan Owens has captured with clarity, wisdom, and graciousness the pathway to authentic Christianity as revealed in the book of James. A must read for every Christian.*

—DR. RICH ROLLINS
EXECUTIVE PASTOR, VALLEY BIBLE CHURCH, HERCULES, CALIFORNIA

*Dan Owens's book left me already anticipating his next one! Grab a chair, pen, and an open heart to devour this book! Dan Owens will fill your heart and mind with a faith that is fueled for the journey.*

—SCOTT DAWSON
AUTHOR OF *THE COMPLETE EVANGELISM GUIDEBOOK*

A Faith That Is Real *provides a strong message to those of us who wish to know the Lord so much better...so much more deeply. Dan Owens has blessed us with a delightful collection of thoughts to ponder and absorb as we continue in our walk with God.*

—GREG POTZER
DIRECTOR, THIS DAY'S THOUGHT

*Dan Owens cracks open the book of James to help us answer the most important question of our lives: Are we, or are we not, authentic followers of Jesus Christ? In this simple, yet profound work, Owens offers practical insight to the challenge of living in the world, but not of the world.* A Faith That Is Real *reminds us through the impassioned words of James that true happiness is not found within the plans that we make for ourselves, rather it is found in the realization and acceptance of God's purpose in our lives.*

—THEO CHALGREN
EXECUTIVE PRODUCER, HONEST TO GOD! MEDIA

*In* A Faith That Is Real, *Dan Owens puts shoe leather on the words of James and brings the timeless biblical theme of authentic Christian faith into the 21st century—without compromising the original meaning to make it fit in with our postmodern culture. Owens brings truth to life in a way that is relevant, understandable, and ultimately life-changing.*

—JOCELYN C. GREEN
CONTRIBUTOR TO *HIGH DEFINITION LIFE, STUDENT EDITION*

*I really enjoyed Owens's book. He has a very fun and accessible style, full of real-life stories that engage the reader. Owens has the ability to preserve the intensity of James' challenging message, while delivering it through a channel that demonstrates the love of God—and makes it practical for life in the everyday world.*

—STEVE THOMASON
DIRECTOR, HART HAUS

A Faith That Is Real *brings the book of James to life! With careful study, relevant illustrations, and practical application, Dan Owens has opened up the Scriptures in a fresh way. Read it. Grab hold of the challenge and live with a faith that is real.*

—JOSE ZAYAS
AUTHOR OF *AIRBORNE: GETTING YOUR FAITH OFF THE GROUND*

*If we are to win our world for Christ, then those who need to experience the Gospel must see authentic Christ followers—and not hyphenated Christians—in each of us who claim his name. Dan Owens gives us practical application from the most practical book of the Bible to challenge us to move beyond pretend Christianity and to follow Jesus Christ wholeheartedly. This book should be on the required reading list for anyone who wants a genuine walk with God.*

—REV. J. R. WHITBY
PRESIDENT/CEO, GOSPEL COMMUNICATIONS INTERNATIONAL

*If you are looking for down-to-earth insights and life-changing principles illustrated by an author living the authentic faith and written in an easy-to-read style, then* A Faith That Is Real *is a book that will inspire you.*

—DR. DONALD BRAKE
VICE PRESIDENT AND DEAN, MULTNOMAH BIBLICAL SEMINARY

A Faith That Is Real *is practical, forceful and useful—much like the book of James itself. When I came to Christ, James was the first New Testament book I read. Those fiercely pragmatic words changed my life. To this day, almost every time I read the Scripture publicly, I conclude with the admonition and prayer that "we will be more than mere hearers of the Word, but doers, also." That, of course, is what makes faith real.*

—KEITH POTTER
SENIOR PASTOR, SARATOGA FEDERATED CHURCH

FOREWORD BY LUIS PALAU

# A
# FAITH
## THAT IS REAL

### DANIEL OWENS

Victor® is an imprint of
Cook Communications Ministries, Colorado Springs, Colorado 80918
Cook Communications, Paris, Ontario
Kingsway Communications, Eastbourne, England

A FAITH THAT IS REAL
© 2006 by Daniel Owens.

Cover Design: Greg Jackson, Thinkpen Design, llc

Printed in the United States of America.

1 2 3 4 5 6 7 8 9 10 Printing / Year 11 10 09 08 07 06

Library of Congress Cataloging-in-Publication Data

Owens, Daniel, 1956-
  A faith that is real / by Daniel Owens.
     p. cm.
  Includes bibliographical references.
  ISBN 0-7814-4186-2
  1. Bible. N.T. James--Criticism, interpretation, etc. I. Title.
  BS2785.52.O94 2005
  227'.9107--dc22
                              2005030275

*To the Fair Oaks Church family, who allowed me to express my thoughts and feelings with transparency and confidence. Through you the Lord helped build my faith, and Jesus became more real to me. Thank you!*

# CONTENTS

# Foreword

*BY Luis Palau*

A re you ready to be real?
   I love encouraging other Christians to embrace a more authentic faith in Jesus Christ. Sure, as an evangelist my passion is to win as many people as possible to Jesus Christ. That's a call God has given me. But coming to Jesus Christ is only the beginning. God has much in store for each of his children!

What keeps you from being real? The expectations of others? Your own desires?

God does not ask us to put on a show and masquerade as if we were "good" Christians. This life is not about being perfect. Rather than depend on our human efforts to live the Christian life, you and I have the privilege of dwelling in Jesus Christ and letting him do his work through us. Jesus Christ and the Holy Spirit are God's gift to us for living this life!

You and I can enjoy authentic living only when we take off our masks and allow Jesus Christ to make us the kind of people he wants us to be. Letting our weaknesses show gives new meaning to the verse, "When I am weak, then I am strong" (2 Corinthians 12:10). We can spread the fragrance of Christ only when we live out our Christian walk so that the world can see who he is through us.

I have seen this truth clearly demonstrated when we have held conferences for young Christian leaders. You would think they would be eager to hear some of the great "secrets of success." But do you know what encourages them most? The same thing that would probably encourage you: hearing that I struggle, just as they struggle; knowing that I too must (not just can, but must!) depend fully on God to help me through my ups and downs, my disappointments and failures. They see that God never rewards me for putting on a good show of perfection. Instead, he uses me in and through my weaknesses.

As I am honest with these young men and women, they take courage that being real, blemishes and all, doesn't make them any less useful to God. In fact, being real about our failures opens the way for God to truly work in and through us. Authenticity and humility go hand in hand. God delights in raising and blessing the humble.

We don't have to pretend that Jesus Christ lives in us; he *does* live in us. We don't have to put on a pretty, spiritual-looking covering. When we live honestly and transparently in the indwelling glory of Christ, people will see our weaknesses. But they will also see beyond our weaknesses and witness the reality of Jesus in our lives.

The rich, wonderful, and powerful book of James urges Christians to embrace a more authentic faith. My good friend Dan Owens' book will challenge you to do the same.

Read this book with an open Bible and an expectant heart!

*Luis Palau is a world-renowned evangelist,*
*broadcaster, and author of* Stop Pretending
*(NexGen, Cook Communications, 2003).*

# ACKNOWLEDGMENTS

I would like to express my deep gratitude to Fair Oaks Church, where I had the privilege of first presenting the life-transforming messages contained in this book.

My wholehearted thanks to Carl Dawson, who has been a "Barnabas" as we have served together with Eternity Minded Ministries around the world. Carl, your hard work, dedication, and genuine faith have been an inspiration to me.

Thanks to Karen Weitzel for typing the first draft of my manuscript—no easy task! My sincere thanks to David Sanford, president of Sanford Communications, Inc., who helped turn my publishing dream into a reality. As well, special thanks to SCI associate editors Elizabeth Ries Jones and Elizabeth Honeycutt, who helped polish each chapter and added the application questions.

Finally, I want to thank Craig Bubeck, who believed in the message of this book and encouraged me to write it. Craig, I am very much looking forward to working with you on several more books in the near future.

My prayer is that this book will enrich the faith of many thousands of readers for God's glory, honor, and praise.

# INTRODUCTION

What is bugging James, the half brother of Jesus?
Even with a quick read of the Bible book bearing his name, one cannot escape the passionate tone and in-your-face language with which James communicates to his audience. His fervor floods the pages, conveying an intensity borne out of his love for the people he is addressing and his desire for them to live as true followers of God.

James certainly isn't gushing warm fuzzies. Making the reader feel good is not his main concern! Instead, James asks twenty powerful questions and issues nearly fifty imperatives reminding other Christians of the appropriate actions and responses of believers in Jesus Christ. The string of warnings and encouragements that James gives helps to clue us in as to what was troubling him.

His concern, in one word, is pretense. Repeatedly, James warns Christians to check their lives to see if their faith is real or if they are just pretending.

These Jewish Christians to whom James penned his letter were contemporaries of Jesus. They had walked alongside of him, had heard his teaching, and had watched him perform miracles. Many of them had witnessed his death, resurrection, and ascension into heaven. They understood who Jesus was and trusted him as their Messiah. They became the first believers, the first church. Yet as little as ten to thirty years later, these first-generation believers were no longer living as followers of Jesus Christ.

Though claiming the name of Christ, the first-century church was conducting itself like the world around it—giving preferential treatment to the wealthy, showing indifference to the poor, allowing uncontrolled speech, displaying a critical spirit, holding on to selfish ambition, listening to worldly wisdom. James uses his letter to warn the Christians of the early church about the dangers of faking Christianity, of allowing society to dictate what they do and how they behave.

He seems to be saying, "You were witnesses to the greatest event in history: the death, resurrection, and ascension of the Son of God. Jesus died for your sins, you trusted him to save you, and you claim to be his followers. How, then, can you love the world like this? Don't you know that friendship with the world is hatred toward God?"

His concern echoes the words of Jesus recorded in what we now know as the Sermon on the Mount:

> Not everyone who says to me, "Lord, Lord," will enter the kingdom of heaven, but only he who does the will of my Father who is in heaven. Many will say to me on that day, "Lord, Lord, did we not prophesy in your name, and in your name drive out demons and perform many miracles?" Then I will tell them plainly, "I never knew you. Away from me, you evildoers!" (Matthew 7:21–23)

The first time I traveled to Singapore, at the invitation of that island nation's Christian leaders, I spent some time sightseeing and visited one of their famous shopping centers. From the moment I walked in to the moment I left, I kept hearing one little phrase: "copy watch."

I discovered that many Singapore shopkeepers sell copies of Rolex watches. These watches are gorgeous, exact replicas of a four-thousand-dollar Rolex, but they cost only twenty-five to thirty dollars. For that money, the buyer receives not only a great-looking watch, but also a box inscribed with the Rolex logo and a certificate of authenticity. The only problem is that the watch isn't genuine. It's counterfeit, and the Rolex company won't honor any warranty on it because the watch isn't theirs. It's a "copy watch."

Rolex values authenticity in its watches. How much more does God value authentic Christianity in his followers? God wants us to examine our lives to make sure our faith isn't a copy. Our fake religion looks good on the outside—proudly wearing the Christian logo on our necks, attending church each Sunday, and carrying around our certificate of authenticity: the Bible. But what do our lives really say? Are we just pretending?

I think if James were around today, he would say that many Christians in the United States are "copy Christians." He would pull out his Palm Pilot, type the same letter, and e-mail it to churches across America. The strong words he issued to his contemporaries are just as relevant for us today.

Author Charles Templeton said of America, "The statistical columns reveal a nation increasingly Christian. The news columns reveal a mounting paganism."[1]

Approximately 85 percent of Americans identify themselves as Christians, according to the Gallup and Barna's surveys.[2] But how many truly follow Jesus Christ's teachings? With all the people who go to church on Sunday morning and claim to be followers of Jesus, why are we not seeing a greater impact within our own society? I dare say that if half as many who claim Christianity actually lived it, our nation would be changed dramatically and, even more important, our lives would be altered drastically.

Author and theologian C. S. Lewis called people whose lives aren't changed by Jesus "hyphenated Christians." By adding the word *Christian* to whatever they do—no matter whether it's moral or immoral, decent or indecent—they think God will bless them and everything will turn out swell.

I read an article about a woman from Texas who called herself a "Christian stripper." She said, "That's what I do to the glory of God." Talk about a hyphenated Christian!

Yet many of us behave in similar ways. We say, "Yes, I'm a follower of Jesus, but this particular sin is part of who I am. Jesus can use me even if I swear occasionally or cheat my boss out of a few minutes at break time or treat the poor disrespectfully. That's just the way life is. God understands." We tend to take whatever we want to do, however we choose to live, whatever our personality flaws are, and add them onto the word *Christian*. We believe that makes everything okay.

My brother, my sister, great danger exists in thinking and acting this way. D. L. Moody, the great evangelist, said that Christians are like ships on the open sea trying to stay afloat. We float on the sea of the world, and if the world begins to seep into the ship, we begin to change. If too much of the world floods our ship, we begin to sink.

That is why James expounded so passionately in this book. He saw worldliness creeping into the church. He watched Christians calling themselves one thing, but acting like something else. The pretense greatly troubled him.

James knew that being a disciple of Jesus Christ was more than just calling oneself by a certain name or associating with certain people. This viewpoint was also held by other disciples of Christ, as we see in 1 John 2:5–6, "This is how we know we are in him: Whoever claims to live in him [that is, in Jesus] must walk as Jesus did."

The word *walk* in this passage literally means "a habitual course of life." That is not to say that we will never fail. But as a consistent routine we should check our speech, our actions, our thoughts, and our responses against the way Jesus would speak, act, think, and respond. Then we should correct those areas that don't measure up. If we walk through life without giving a second thought to what Jesus would do, we are heading for disaster. Our ship is taking on water, and we are going to sink.

Fortunately, God provides us with warnings when we are aboard a sinking vessel. Through the prodding of his Holy Spirit, he graciously provokes us to return to him, to give up the pretense and be real again.

It has happened to me. The Holy Spirit stirred up feelings of dissatisfaction about my Christian experience and caused me to long for more honesty in my Christian walk. He helped me recognize that what I said to others didn't quite match up with what I was experiencing, that I was inviting people to have a personal relationship with God but was far away from him myself.

How about you? You say you are a follower of Jesus, but is Jesus real to you? Are you going through the motions, doing good things, performing as expected, but really living for yourself?

As we study the book of James, my desire is that we will look at our lives in light of the teachings of James and Jesus and ask, "Is this something I'm experiencing, or has the world told me what to do and what to believe? Am I doing what the world wants me to do more than I am doing what Jesus wants me to do?"

Remember, the greatest issue is not what others think about us. The greatest issue is what God thinks about our lives and our walks with him.

As we go through this study of James, I pray that at the end you will be able to say, "Yes, Jesus is real to me," for that is the greatest desire of his heart.

God desires to
develop us into all we
can be for his glory,
and one way he
accomplishes that
desire is through trials.

# AN UNNATURAL RESPONSE TO NATURAL EVENTS

## JAMES 1:1–4

A well-known saying in the biking world states there are two kinds of motorcyclists: those who have gone down, and those who are going to go down. Crashes are bound to happen in biking. Whether riders are experts or novices, old or young, straddling a Harley-Davidson or a Heinz 57 pieced together in the garage, all will crash at some point in their riding career.

Christians could have a similar saying. Two types of believers exist: those who have already experienced trials, and those who will experience them in the future. No one in this life is exempt from troubles and heartache. A carefree, trial-less existence is nothing less than impossible.

Thomas Jefferson said, "The goal of life is the avoidance of pain."[1] Sorry, Mr. President, but life doesn't work that way. Pain, suffering, misery, and trials will definitely arise in everyone's lifetime. They can't be avoided.

That truth doesn't change once a person gives his heart to the Lord. I have heard believers say, "Come to Jesus, and everything will be wonderful." Coming to Jesus is a wonderful thing, but that decision doesn't mean that everything from that point on will be wonderful. No place in the Bible do we read, "If you have Jesus in your heart, you're not going to have a single problem. Life will be great. The sun will always shine; you won't have any pain or problems."

In fact, the opposite is true. Jesus told his disciples, "If they persecuted me, they will persecute you also" (John 15:20). And Paul wrote, "For it has been granted to you on behalf of Christ not only to believe on him, but also to suffer for him" (Philippians 1:29), and, "Everyone who wants to live a godly life in Christ Jesus will be persecuted" (2 Timothy 3:12).

Throughout history, persecution has been an Equal Opportunity Employer. Trials come to pastor and parishioner alike, without regard to age, socioeconomic background, race, or religious affiliation.

## God Uses Trials to Make Us Joyful

The believers to whom James penned his letter certainly were experiencing adversity. They had fled Jerusalem, their home, after the martyrdom of Stephen and the escalating persecution of Christians (see Acts 6:8—8:3). The people scattered throughout Palestine, some traveling as far as Phoenicia, Cyprus, and Syrian Antioch. According to historians, they were suffering through a severe economic downturn resulting from lingering drought. Tension caused by political, social, and religious unrest filled the air. Not long after James wrote this letter, the Jews waged war against Rome (AD 66–70).

Times were hard. James knew that these Christians were in the middle of difficult circumstances. He wanted to remind them that though trials were inevitable, they could choose how they were going to respond to those difficult times. He told his readers, "Consider it pure joy, my brothers, whenever you face trials of many kinds" (1:2).

The word *consider* in this verse is an imperative and indicates an immediate action. It's as though James is telling them: "Do it now. Once and for all, cement this truth in your mind. Choose, through an act of your will, to consider these trials pure joy."

The term *pure joy* means joy unmixed with any other emotions. What James was saying is this: "During a trial, choose joy—don't contaminate that mind-set by mixing it with fear or worry or unrest. Your attitude should be one of pure, unadulterated joy."

Let's be honest here. Joy is not the usual response whenever adversity strikes. If we lose our jobs, we don't say, "Wonderful, I'm unemployed! I'm having the greatest time in life right now." No, we tend to think in terms of fight or flight. Either we want to push against it, to manipulate it, or we want to run from it, to get as far from it as we can.

Counting our trials as pure joy is not natural, which I think is the point James is trying to make. We can't pretend to have this uncontaminated, unadulterated joy. It can't be faked. The joy James speaks of is a supernatural response produced by the Holy Spirit who lives inside of every believer. He produces in us much more than a happy-go-lucky, laughter-filled, smile-at-life existence. The joy he gives birth to is more of a sense of triumph, a deep-down knowing that God is working everything for our good—even the hardships we are enduring (see Romans 8:28).

I believe that is why James reminds his readers to whom they belong. In his introductory statement, he calls himself "a servant of God" (1:1). A servant doesn't tell his master what he should do or what he needs to do; he trusts his master to do what is best. James knew that God is seated on his throne and is in control of every situation. He is never caught off guard by any trial a believer may endure.

## God Uses Trials to Train and Discipline Us

I think it is important to realize that in this section of verses, James does not use the word *trial* synonymously with *temptation*, as was done in the King James Version of this passage. He deals with inner moral trials later (see 1:13–15). Neither is James talking about the hardships we bring upon ourselves because of poor decisions or wrong choices. A student who flunks a test because he failed to study is not enduring a trial but is simply living out the consequence of his bad decision.

The word James uses for *trial* in this passage literally means adversity. Hard times—sicknesses, accidents, disappointments, persecution, death—often come out of nowhere. Usually they are not expected nor are they caused to happen; they just occur.

When we are struck with such an unexpected, unprovoked trial, we can be assured that God is using it to develop his character in us. James tells us, "You know that the testing of your faith develops perseverance" (1:3). Picture the process gold or silver must go through to be refined. James uses that same word for *testing* in this passage.[2] God uses this process to purify and strengthen us. James says to count our trials as pure joy because God is at work in our lives doing something amazing.

The United States Navy docks several of its aircraft carriers in San Diego Bay. I recently took a tour on one, the USS *Abraham Lincoln*. Costing billions of dollars to build, the carrier accommodates more than fifty aircraft, two nuclear reactors, and five thousand crew members. It resembles an entire city with ATMs, bowling alleys, and a surgical hospital. During a visit to the bridge where the captain issues orders, I saw who "drives" that multibillion-dollar ship with who-knows-how-many dollars of aircraft on the deck. Some nineteen-year-old kid! I am concerned every time my teenager drives my car, and the captain of that ship trusts one to navigate his carrier. That's because the navy took that young man or woman through intense times of training. Only after coming out the other side, after successfully completing those training exercises, was that young person stationed on the bridge of that ship.

Similarly, God uses trials as training exercises in our lives, as discipline to develop his character in us.

The Bible shows God using discipline in three ways. Corrective discipline is what God uses to get our attention when we have sinned against him. David experienced God's corrective discipline when he slept with Bathsheba, another man's wife, and was rebuked by Nathan the prophet (see 2 Samuel 11—12). James is speaking of adversity in this passage. Still, I believe we can be joyful when receiving God's corrective discipline because it validates our relationship as a son or daughter of God (see Hebrews 12:5–8) and turns us from a destructive path to the way he would have us go (see 1 Corinthians 11:32; 2 Corinthians 7:10).

Another form of discipline is preventative discipline. God uses preventative discipline to keep us from doing something that he knows is going to hurt us. For example, Paul was given "a thorn in the flesh" to keep him from being proud (see 2 Corinthians 12:7–10).

The last type of discipline is educational discipline. God sometimes disciplines us to reveal a characteristic or trait about himself of which we are not aware. Job received educational discipline through his multitude of trials and in the end cried out to God, "I know that you can do all things; no plan of yours can be thwarted" (Job 42:2).

We can count our trials as pure joy because we know that God will use them to mold us into the people he wants us to be. Our trials are being used as discipline in our lives for our good.

## God Uses Trials to Prove Our Faith

Trials also reveal the solidity of our faith. James tells us, "Testing … develops perseverance. Perseverance must finish its work so that you may be mature and complete, not lacking anything" (1:3–4). True faith does not dissolve in the presence of adversity. It grows. It endures. Trials are not stumbling blocks; they are stepping stones taking us to a place of maturity.

William Barclay, world-renowned Bible commentator and minister of the Church of Scotland, wrote, "The thing which amazed the heathen in centuries of persecution was that the martyrs did not die grimly. They died singing."[3]

How can people staring death in the face accept it with joy? I believe they can do so because they have learned to see the big picture. They have learned to keep one eye on earth and the other eye on heaven.

When a trial comes, if all we focus on are the transitory things—our world, our lives, our jobs, our homes, our families, our money—we are going to be overwhelmed, agitated, worried, and distressed. But if we focus on the eternal, we can consider the end result God has planned for us and rejoice.

The apostle Paul wrote, "For our light and momentary troubles are achieving for us an eternal glory that far outweighs them all"

(2 Corinthians 4:17). Paul viewed all his trials—and he had quite the list, as we see in 2 Corinthians 11:23–28—as less than nothing when compared to what was waiting for him in heaven. Like Paul, we must keep one eye trained on heaven at all times.

## God Uses Trials to Develop Our Character

The army's great advertising slogan used to be, "Be all that you can be ... in the army." In other words, "Let the army develop your potential." But if you go and sign up for the army today, you are going to have to endure a few things before you become all you can be. You are going to have to physically exert yourself in ways you probably have never done before. You are going to have somebody screaming in your face while you stand unmoving at attention. You are going to be ordered to do things that make no sense whatsoever, and you are going to follow those commands while someone is yelling at you. In the end, after enduring all that and more, you will come out a soldier.

God desires to develop us into all we can be for his glory, and one way he accomplishes that desire is through trials. Will we accept his discipline and respond to trials with joy? Will we draw closer to God, or will we abandon him? Will we say, "Forget it. This is not what I bargained for. I thought the Christian life was going to be fun, everything was going to be great, and everybody was going to love me all the time. I'm calling it quits"? Or will we view our trials as the means God uses to draw us closer to him and say, "Yes, Lord, I accept the trial. I want to learn whatever you want to teach me through this situation"?

Oswald Chambers said, "It is not that you have God but that he has got you. He is at work bending, breaking, molding, and doing just as he chooses. He is doing it for one purpose, that he might be able to say, 'This is my man. This is my woman.'"4

That is God's ultimate purpose in trials, and that is why we can count them pure joy.

## CHAPTER 2

# WISDOM! WHO NEEDS IT?

## JAMES 1:5–8

A bride and groom have just returned from their honeymoon. The bride excitedly prepares her first meal for her husband, a beautiful candlelit dinner. She has informed him that there are two things she cooks very well—apple pie and vegetable lasagna. He takes a bite, chews thoughtfully, and asks, "Which is this?"

We could all stand to exercise a little more wisdom in our lives. So far in James we have already looked at trials, how to deal with them, and what God is doing through them. Now we will look at the need for wisdom in going through these trials, and the need to understand our trials from God's perspective.

## Wisdom in Trials

What is wisdom? Wisdom is the practical use of knowledge. It is not only having knowledge, but also knowing how to use it. Wisdom is an incredibly powerful force that helps us to make right decisions and keeps us from failures that would destroy us.

When do we need wisdom? James instructs us to ask God for wisdom when we are going through a trial. In the midst of a difficult situation, we can simply cry out to the Lord.

Wisdom is quite different from advice. When we ask for advice, we have usually already made up our minds and are just looking for someone to validate our decisions. If a person doesn't give the advice we are looking for, we just ignore it. In the same way, we rarely go to God and say, "Lord, I really don't care how this decision will affect me, or how much stress and suffering it may cause, I just want to do what you want me to do." Rather, we have usually already figured out in our heads what we are going to do, and what we are really thinking is, "God, here's the path I'm going to take. Will you bless my choice and help me as I go?"

What God desires from us is that emptiness that genuinely seeks out his wisdom. We can read the Bible until we are blue in the face and memorize hundreds of verses, but unless we recognize the will of God and do it, it won't make us wise.

One time my dad said to me, "I wish all these books on raising kids had been around when I was raising you." True, there are more books today on raising children; however, reading a parenting book every day will not make us wise parents. We have to take knowledge and apply it to our situations. That is the kind of wisdom James is talking about—the wisdom that allows us to take information and process it in a way that is beneficial and useful.

Wisdom is taking knowledge and knowing how to apply it to our lives. The Bible commands us to pursue wisdom, to seek it out (see Proverbs 4:5–7). Each one of us needs wisdom. Wisdom centers our lives. That doesn't mean we are going to have all the answers, but it does allow us to focus on who God is and what he is doing in our lives—which is molding us into the people he wants us to be.

## Asking for Wisdom

In verse 5 James says, "If any of you lacks wisdom, he should ask God, who gives generously to all without finding fault, and it will be given to him." The Greek word translated *ask* in this verse implies that we are *to keep on asking*. Wisdom should be asked for on a regular basis. God doesn't tire, and neither should we. Asking for wisdom is a habit that is formed by constant use.

When you are in a trial, to whom do you go first—to a friend, to your family, to your coworkers? Remember, the trials James is speaking of here are not trials you have created, but trials that God has allowed to come into your life. God wants you to go to *him* first. He is waiting for you to open up your heart and listen.

The question is not about how great your desire is to *know* God's will, but how great your desire is to *do* it. Are you asking God to give you advice, or wisdom? Are you really saying, "God, tell me what you want me to do, and if I like it, I'll do it"? We have all become so used to making decisions based on our own preferences and opinions that we don't really seek God's wisdom and direction. Do we really want what God wants for us; do we really want God's will in our lives?

While I was doing ministry work in India, I heard a story told of Gandhi. One day someone came to Mahatma Gandhi and said, "I want to know God." Gandhi walked him over to the edge of the river and said, "Let's get into the water." Once they were in, Gandhi took the man's head and held it under water. Gandhi continued to hold on while he struggled, then, just as the man was about to give up, Gandhi lifted his head up out of the water and said, "When you want to know God as desperately as you wanted to breathe just now, then you will find him."

Do you desire God in your life? Do you desire his wisdom? Or do you already have your life planned out? Your heavenly Father is waiting for you—but do you really want him?

## Wisdom Depends on Faith

According to James, wisdom is given to us in return for our faith. He tells us that if we truly want wisdom, God will give it to us, no matter who we are. He gives generously without finding fault. But, James continues in verse 6, he who asks must believe and not doubt. Faith is the key; without it, it is impossible to please God (see Hebrews 11:6).

In the movie *Indiana Jones and the Last Crusade*, one scene stood out to me. Indiana Jones and his dad, along with several others, were searching for the Holy Grail, which they believed could give them eternal life. When they finally reached the mountain where the Holy Grail was believed to be hidden, the villains showed up and shot Indiana Jones' dad. The only hope to save him was to find the Holy Grail, so that he could drink from it and live.

In order to reach the cup, Indiana Jones had to go through

several tests, each of which could end his life. For the third test, Jones was standing in a dark cave with a giant ravine in front of him. The trick was that the bridge that spanned the chasm had been painted the same color as the ravine, and it appeared to Jones that one step would mean certain death. This bridge was about six inches below the ledge on which Jones was standing, so he could neither see it nor feel it until he stepped out in faith. He then made it safely to the other side.

Has God asked you to take a step of faith? In this passage James is saying that without faith, we cannot expect to gain wisdom. God is asking us to trust his promises, because he loves us and has our best interests in mind. We need faith to exercise wisdom—wisdom to endure, and to give us strength for difficult times.

## Wisdom to See

Helen Keller, a blind and deaf woman with remarkable intelligence, wrote an article many years ago entitled "Three Days to See." In it she described what she would like to look at if she could have three days of sight. She said, "If I can get so much pleasure from mere touch, how much more beauty must be revealed by sight.... Perhaps I can best illustrate by imagining what I should most like to see if I were given the use of my eyes, say, for just three days."

On the first day, she wrote, she would see people—all the friends who had taken care of her through the years. She wanted to see their smiling faces and tender eyes. Then, in the afternoon, she would take a walk in the forest, enjoying the beautiful sights of nature and the glory of a colorful sunset.

The second day she said she would rise early to see a thrilling miracle: the process of night being transformed into day—something she had never been able to see before. She would then make her way to the museums where she could see paintings and sculptures that she had previously only been able to feel.

On the third day she would rise up early again and go to the city where she would see the skyscrapers, the traffic, and all the people. In the evening she would attend the theater or the movies. As she concluded her article, she offered this advice, "I who am blind can give one hint to those who see.... Use your eyes as if tomorrow you would be stricken blind.... Then, at last, you would really see, and a new world of beauty would open itself before you."[1]

We must ask for wisdom to be able to see God at work. However, wisdom can be halted by our divided hearts. Again, in verses 6 through 8 James says, "But when he asks, he must believe and not doubt, because he who doubts is like a wave of the sea, blown and tossed by the wind. That man should not think he will receive anything from the Lord; he is a double-minded man, unstable in all he does."

This passage, like many others, has a qualifier. In it James is saying, "God will give you wisdom, but your heart cannot be divided. You cannot say, 'I love this world and everything in it and its value system and everything it has for me, and God, at the same time I kind of love you too.'" In order for God to give us wisdom, we must act in faith, and we must value our relationship with him as more important than anything else in this world. God does not like lukewarm Christianity (see Revelation 3:14–16).

I ask you again. Is it real? Is your faith real? Or do you have a divided heart? James says that if you have a divided heart, you are going to be unstable. You cannot fool God; and you cannot hide your heart from him. He knows whether your heart is divided or whether it is completely his.

God is asking you: "Do you want us to be friends? Do you want me in your life?" It's all about the heart. God is waiting for you to step out in faith, faith that says: "God, I believe you exist; I believe you love me. Lord, I need you in my life." When you step out in faith and ask for his wisdom, God will give it to you.

Ask God to grant you the desire to want him above all other things. Ask him to let you see life from his perspective. Ask him for the wisdom you need to go through this life in a way that will bring glory to his name.

James wants to remind us that God is more important than anything we might own, dearer to us than any possession.

## CHAPTER 3

# CAUGHT BETWEEN TWO WORLDS
### JAMES 1:9–11

A man is getting ready to complete his final test for a parachuting class. To graduate, he must jump out of the plane and parachute to the ground by himself. He takes the leap; as he is falling toward the earth, he remembers the instructions. He calmly counts to ten, and then pulls the cord. Nothing happens. He tries the auxiliary cord to open the reserve chute. Again, nothing. He begins to panic as he falls faster and faster toward the earth.

Suddenly he notices someone flying up toward him from the ground. Although this seems very strange, he calls out to him, "Hey, do you know anything about parachutes?"

The other guy yells back, "No. Do you know anything about lighting a gas stove?"

We get into similar situations economically. Sometimes we are going up; sometimes we are coming down. The question is whether or not we are at peace in our circumstances. As you think about your life and your economic outlook, are you at peace with your situation?

## Wealth Doesn't Determine Our Position before God

We like to have our lives all planned out. We are going to accomplish this, we are going to have that kind of family, we are going to accumulate this much stuff, then we are going to retire and enjoy life. Do we ever think about the end and what's going to happen then? In this passage of Scripture, James says that people of humble circumstances should take pride in their high position. Does that mean that God wants everybody to be poor? What is he talking about?

In America, we look down on being poor. If a person is living in humble circumstances, we tell him that he can do better than that. We tell him to work the system and get himself to a better place in life.

You may remember that these Christians were very poor, not only economically, but also socially. The phrase "humble circumstances" means that they were on the bottom rung of the socioeconomic ladder of that day. People looked down on them; they were ostracized. These Christians were not poor because they were lazy or because they lacked ambition, but because they were persecuted by the Roman government and by the community in which they lived.

Rome was actually very tolerant of foreigners, as long as they paid homage to Caesar. But the Christians created an entirely new problem. At first some of the Romans thought that Christianity was just a sect of Judaism. The Jews were okay because they didn't really bother anyone—they kept to themselves and didn't try to bring anyone into their faith. The Christians, however, wanted to tell everyone about Jesus until the entire empire converted. They refused to worship the emperor, they would not sacrifice to the Roman gods, and they would not attend the gladiator games. They would not throw away unhealthy babies as they were instructed, and they treated slaves with kindness. So they were heavily persecuted.

In this passage James is saying to these people, "Yes, you're poor, and you're being persecuted, but take pride in your high position." The word *pride* here is not pride in the sense of self-importance. It is pride in the sense of being joyful about belonging to God's family.

## God Is More Important than Our Wealth

I once met a man who was extremely wealthy. He had made his money in oil, and was a man of great stature in the state of Texas. He had private planes, houses all over the country, household servants, butlers, and chauffeurs. He had a lot of worldly wealth.

In the recession of the early 1990s, he lost everything. He lost the limousines, the private jets, the servants, and a lot of friends who were sticking with him because of his great wealth. Even after he had lost so much, he held his head high when he walked into a room full of businessmen. He shook hands with the same confidence he always had.

As we sat down for a meeting, I listened to this man speak joyfully about his life. Although he had lost so much and was now living in an apartment, he had joy because he knew he was a child of the King. Losing his wealth hadn't changed the most important thing in his life—his position with God.

I wonder, as we look at our lives, if we view God as more important than all other things. It is possible to go from great wealth to great poverty in this life. If that happened to us, could we say: "I came into this world with nothing, and I'm leaving with nothing, but hallelujah, God is still my Father!"?

You may be going through a difficult time right now. You may have lost a job or perhaps you are having a hard time financially. You can take comfort in your position with God. Don't forget to whom you belong. Even if everything is stripped away from you, may you be able to say as the prophet said, "Yet I will rejoice in the LORD, I will be joyful in God my Savior" (Habakkuk 3:18).

James wants to remind us that God is more important than anything we might own, dearer to us than any possession. We can rejoice in trials, even ones that cause us to lose worldly riches, because God knows us and loves us, and he will not forsake us.

## God Can Use Our Wealth

Sophie Tucker, the old African-American gospel singer, used to say, "I've been rich, and I've been poor, and honey, rich is much better." Many people think that way.

Am I saying that God is against rich Christians? Not at all. Does God love the poor more than he loves the rich? I don't think so. Does God want every Christian to be poor? I don't see that in the Bible. I would say, however, that we must be very careful with the money that we do have. We should use great wisdom in how we spend our money. We can't give away what we don't have. If we don't have anything ourselves, how can we help out anybody else?

One time I spent several weeks with Jerry Colangelo, the owner of the Phoenix Suns. While working with him on a project, I got to stay in his home, interview him, meet his staff, and work in his office. Jerry does some wonderful work in the city of Phoenix, giving away money to the poor and homeless.

There is no question in my mind that God has blessed some people with the gift of making money. I have been a recipient of that gift. Many people have written checks to Eternity Minded Ministries through the years—sometimes $1,000, sometimes $10,000 or even $50,000. One time a man said to me, "I don't have any of the gifts you have. I can't preach, and no one comes to the Lord when I talk, but I can do this. I can make money and help you get where you need to be so that you can win people for the Lord."

Money is not evil in itself. God is not against wealth. He is against the hoarding of wealth. Jesus said, "You cannot serve both God and Money" (Matthew 6:24). But if you use money for a tool, it can be wonderful. Just remember that life is more than possessions. If all your happiness, joy, and contentment are wrapped up in something that you own, you are on shifting sand.

Psalm 49:16–17 says, "Do not be overawed when a man grows rich, when the splendor of his house increases; for he will take nothing with him when he dies, his splendor will not descend with him." In the same way, James is warning us to be careful about the role money plays in our lives.

## God Wants Us to Use Our Wealth Wisely

Several years ago, I spoke at a retirement party for a CEO. One thing that he said has stuck with me. As he looked at all the young executives around him, he said, "I know each of you wants my job, and I'll tell you how to get it. Last week my daughter was married and as I walked her down the aisle, I realized that I didn't really know her. I didn't know the name of her best friend or the last book she had read or her favorite color. That's the price I paid to get this job. If you want to pay that price, you can have it."

When money distorts our values, we are in trouble. You do not have to be a victim of the American dream. You do not have to listen to what the world tells you about what to have and what to own in order to be successful. I know of a doctor on the East Coast who lives on 40 percent of his salary and gives away the other 60 percent. He told me, "I don't have to be what a successful doctor is supposed to be. I can do what Jesus wants me to do."

When my kids were young, they used to ask, "Dad, are we rich?" At the time, we were a family of four living on $25,000 a year with one car, and a house with a leaky roof. We didn't have enough pots and pans to catch all the drips of water that came through the roof. One set of grandparents was paying for our boys' preschool. The other set was giving us $250 a month to buy food. Our parents sent us money for gas so we could come visit them. Were we rich? Absolutely; we were filthy rich.

When I visit a family with ten people living in five hundred square feet, when I look out my hotel window and see children rummaging through garbage cans for something to eat, when I see children who are so poor and dirty I feel ashamed that I have money in my pockets, when I see a family who has one blanket for each person and one pot in which to cook their food, I know that I am rich. When I realize that every day tens of thousands of children die of starvation and malnutrition, I feel incredibly rich.

Are you rich? If you bought this book with your own money, you are richer than most of the people in the world. Jesus isn't against wealth, but he wants us to be wise in the way we use it. John Wesley, reflecting on his life, said, "Make all you can, save all you can, give all you can."[1] One day all of us, the rich and the poor, are going to stand before the throne, and God will not only look at what we have done but also at how we have used our resources.

The graveside services are over now. All had left and I was alone.

I began to read the names and dates chiseled there at every stone.

The name showed whether it was a mom or a dad, a daughter or a baby son.

The dates were different but the amount the same. There were two dates on every one.

It was then that I noticed something; it was just a simple line.

It was a dash between those dates and placed there it stood for time.

All at once it dawned on me how important was that little line.

The dates placed there belong to God. But that line is yours and mine.

It's God who gives this precious life and God who takes away.

But that line between he gives to us to do with what we may.

We know God's written the first date down of each and every one.

And we know those hands will write again for the last date has to come.

We know they'll write that last date down quite soon we know for some.

But upon the line between my dates and yours I hope he'll write "Well done."

Author Unknown[2]

God has made each of us responsible for our time and resources. We are living in this world, but what happens here will affect the next world. Are we being followers of Jesus when it comes to our time, our talents, and our treasures that he has given us?

# WHO CAN WE BLAME IT ON?

*JAMES 1:12–13*

One variation of Murphy's Law is: "The person who can smile when things go wrong is the one who has already thought of someone to blame it on."

We are always looking for somebody to blame, and that statement is never truer than when it comes to our sins and failures. So James tells us, "When tempted, no one should say, 'God is tempting me.' For God cannot be tempted by evil, nor does he tempt anyone" (1:13).

As a kid, one of my favorite television programs was the *Flip Wilson Show*. Wilson was a great comedian. One of his lines was, "The devil made me do it," and he gave it in defense of anything he did wrong.

We would like to be able to blame the Devil for everything bad in our lives, but the word *sin* brings us a sense of responsibility. If we have sinned, we have done something wrong, and we are responsible for our actions. In our society, we don't like that. We want to blame our spouses, our children, our employers, or even just the fact that we live in America.

## The Path to Destruction

Temptation wouldn't be such a big deal if we didn't have the issue of sin in our lives. James uses the word several times in his writing, and in this passage, he uses it to mean "to miss the mark." When we sin, we miss the mark that God has established. He has set a target of how we should live, and yet we miss that mark.

*Sin* is a very unpopular word. People get angry and defensive about it. You can talk to them about God's love and all the wonderful things about knowing Jesus, but if you tell them that they are sinners, they get offended. Yet it is still the truth.

A couple years ago I took a test on shooting a handgun. I had to complete a lot of paperwork and then go to the sheriff's department for the test. It was fairly simple. I went down to the basement, put five shells in my gun, and shot at a black circle about fifteen yards away. All five shots had to land in the circle; if I had missed the mark, I would have failed the test.

Sin works the same way. God sets a standard, and when we don't meet that standard, we miss the mark. There is no halfway; either we hit the target, or we miss it.

We have all missed the mark. Most of us don't like to admit it, but we have all sinned. We have satisfied ourselves without thinking of other people. We have lied and cheated. We have had idols and worshipped other gods. We have missed the mark of God's perfection. That's what makes the message of the cross such a glorious thing.

If we think we haven't sinned, we are in a dangerous place (see 1 John 1:8). Or, if we have been in church for so long that we think we are actually a pretty good people, we are also in a dangerous place. We have created in our own minds what a bad sin is and what an okay sin is. Are there sins that God hates more than others?

In Matthew 15:18–20, Jesus said: "But the things that come out of the mouth come from the heart, and these make a man 'unclean.' For out of the heart come evil thoughts, murder, adultery, sexual immorality, theft, false testimony, slander. These are what make a man 'unclean.'"

So often we worry about the external—how we appear to others. We have our lists of things that a good Christian does or does not do. It would be wiser to go back and look at the things Jesus is most concerned about. In Galatians 5:19, Paul wrote, "The acts of the sinful nature are obvious." We don't have to sit and wonder, "Is this a sinful thing or not?" Paul said these are obvious, and in verses 20–21 he listed them: "sexual immorality, impurity and debauchery; idolatry and witchcraft; hatred, discord, jealousy, fits of rage, selfish ambition, dissensions, factions and envy; drunkenness, orgies, and the like."

Many of these are sins that can't be seen from the outside. We can go to church and look like pious Christians, but Jesus said that the sins inside of us can destroy our lives.

Why is temptation such a big deal? Because sin is a big deal. If there was no such thing as sin, we wouldn't worry about being tempted. If gossiping weren't a sin, we wouldn't worry about being tempted to gossip. However, Jesus said that these things that are inside of us are who we really are. Sometimes I look in the mirror, and I may like what I see on the outside, but I don't like what I know is inside. It can be a very frightening thing to face one's own sin.

C. S. Lewis said, "The suddenness of a provocation does not make me an ill-tempered man. It only shows me what an ill-tempered man I already am."[1] That is so true. We can't blame someone else for our sins. It's inside of us already. When we lose our tempers with someone, that person didn't make us mad. That individual just revealed that we are angry people inside. Why? Because we come by sin naturally. As Adam sinned, so we sin. It is our nature to do so.

I remember reading an article in *Time* magazine that said all DNA can be traced back to one person.[2] We all have the same ancestors—Adam and Eve. "Sin entered the world through [them], and death through sin" (Romans 5:12). Our propensity to sin is something that is within us, though that doesn't make it right.

We tend to bash men a lot for being tempted with lust. But in this passage, James is talking about much more than physical desire. He is talking about the whole scope of sin. Not only is he concerned with the sin of lust, he is also concerned with the sin of speech, the sin of presumption, and the sin of being double minded.

James is concerned about our way of life. Is it real? Is our faith real enough to keep us from habitually missing the mark? Sin destroys our joy and hurts our walk with God. Why was James concerned about temptation? Because he knew for certain that if we follow it out to the end, it will destroy our lives.

## God Has No Capacity for Sin

James warns us that when we are tempted, we should not say that God is tempting us, because God can neither tempt nor be tempted. We want to blame God for our failures. Adam did it when he ate of the forbidden fruit in the Garden of Eden. When God asked him if he had done so, he said to God, "Well, *you* were the one who put the woman here with me, and she gave me the fruit" (see Genesis 3:12). He wanted to blame God for putting the woman there to mess everything up. It doesn't work that way, however, because God has no capacity for sin. We can't blame him for our temptations, or for our giving in to them.

In 1646, some people in England got together and drew up the Westminster Confession of Faith. This creed was adopted by the Church of Scotland and then by the Presbyterians. Many denominations still use it today, with some modifications.

The Westminster Confession has one of the most succinct, clearest descriptions of God. It says, "There is but one only, living, and true God, who is infinite in being and perfection, a most pure spirit, invisible, without body, parts, or passions; immutable, immense, eternal, incomprehensible, almighty, most wise, most holy, most free, most absolute."[3]

With God there is no evil passion to be justified. With God there is no power to be gained by manipulation. He has all power. With God there is no money to be gotten by shady dealing. With God there is no happiness to be sought after because he is happy within himself. God is so far beyond us. God is perfectly holy.

In Isaiah 6:1–3, the prophet wrote:

> In the year that King Uzziah died, I saw the Lord seated
> on a throne, high and exalted, and the train of his robe

filled the temple. Above him were seraphs, each with six wings: With two wings they covered their faces, with two they covered their feet, and with two they were flying. And they were calling to one another: "Holy, holy, holy is the LORD Almighty."

We have to understand that God and sin do not live together. God is holy. Even the seraphs, these angelic beings created by God, are covering their faces as they cry "holy, holy, holy." God, in his incredible majesty, lets these seraphs fly around his throne day after day, month after month, year after year, through all eternity, crying out continually, "Holy, holy, holy."

In English, if we want to emphasize a word or point, we use bold font, italics, underlining, or exclamation points. In the Bible, emphasis is indicated by repetition; the more times a word is repeated, the more importance is being communicated. For instance, when Jesus says, "Truly, truly, I say to you," as he does on many occasions in the gospels, he really wants us to listen carefully. This passage from Isaiah is one of the few places where we find a word repeated three times.

God is beyond our limits. He goes beyond our understanding. God is holy—unlike anything else we know or experience. We cannot begin to fathom how different he is, how glorious he is, how holy he is. His holiness encompasses moral purity, ethical beauty, and moral perfection.

When I was thirteen years old, I fell and broke both my arms. I will never forget the feeling of lying there helpless at the bottom of a gully with my arms twisted. I desperately wanted my dad to come find me. He would make everything okay. On the other hand, I had disobeyed him in going there, and I wasn't sure I really wanted him to find me.

In a similar way, the sins in our lives sometimes make us want to run and hide from God. We look at our lives and see our shortcomings, and we are afraid. If God could take every sin, every thought, every attitude, every action—everything we have ever done—and put it on a videotape and give it to us to watch, we would feel pretty bad. Isaiah saw all his sins at one time, and that's why he cried out, "Woe is me" (6:5 KJV).

We do not understand how our sinfulness and God's holiness can come together. It should give us great faith and great joy to understand that God loves us so much that even in our sinfulness he provided a way for us to come to him.

## CHAPTER 5

# THERE IS NO "CATCH AND RELEASE"!
## JAMES 1:13–15

A little boy has accidentally swallowed a penny and is afraid that he is going to die. His mother, attempting to console him, says, "It's okay, sweetheart. The penny will come out sometime." The boy still believes he is going to die, so the mother goes over to her purse, takes out another penny, and pretends to pull it from her son's ear.

"What's this?" she asks. "Look, the penny has already come out your ear."

The little boy is astonished. He grabs the penny from her hand, swallows it, and says, "Mommy, do it again!"

Sometimes we react the same way to temptation. We are tempted by things that are not good for us, but instead of avoiding them, we say, "Do it again; it's all right."

There is no question that temptation is greater today than ever before. We live in a time when temptation bombards us every week, every day, every moment. The intensity is greater, and yielding to temptation is more acceptable than it has ever been before.

Several years ago, I was having dinner with Luis Palau and about six other men. We were discussing this issue of temptation, and Luis told us that it didn't matter how old a person gets, temptation never stops pounding at his door. "I'm in my fifties, and I'm still tempted by some of the same things I was tempted with when I was young," he said. The rest of us, who were in our thirties, were all thinking, *Rats, we thought we were going to outgrow this stuff!*

I read an article about a Christian college president who had embezzled thousands of dollars from the school and spent most of that money on prostitutes. The fact that amazed me was that he was seventy-six years old. We don't outgrow temptation. It is with us our whole lives.

In this passage James is dealing with the temptations that come from within us, from our own evil desires. James is not just talking about sexual lust; he is dealing with all forms of temptation.

I love the "fish terminology" James uses in this passage. I love fishing. There's something about sitting by a river, putting bait on a hook, and watching the fish come along, that gets me excited. One thing I don't like, though, is waiting around for fish to bite. If I have to wait two or three hours, that is not fishing; it is pain. I also don't like "catch and release": catching a fish, looking at it as if to say, "Isn't that a pretty fish?" and then throwing it back into the water. To me, that's not fishing. So I go places where I can actually catch a fish and eat it.

So what does this passage in James have to do with fishing? Well, think of it this way. A little fish is swimming along, having a great day, and doing a little sightseeing. However, this fish is hungry. He is having a "Big Mac attack." He is swimming along doing fine, but he has an inner desire. He is okay at that point; he's just hungry. No harm done … yet.

The same steps that lead a fish to his death are the steps that lead us from temptation to sin.

## The Desire Is within Us

Just like that hungry fish, we have a lustful desire as part of our sinful nature. The word *desire* in this passage refers to the fleshly, illicit desires that we all have within us. These cannot be blamed on God, another person, or the Devil.

We all have temptations. Whether it is to think something wrong, to say something wrong, or to do something wrong, we are all tempted.

I will never forget the day I was shopping in Singapore, looking for presents for my wife and kids. As I walked down the unfamiliar streets, a thought came to my mind that made me stop and catch my breath. I realized that no one in that city knew who I was and that I could do anything I wanted and no one would know. I was thousands of miles from my home, my family, and my church. No one would ever find out. For me, that was the beginning of a new understanding of temptation.

We all face temptation, because we all have those desires, those things within us that James says can literally destroy our lives.

## We Are Lured by Bait

So our little fish is innocently swimming along, when suddenly he spots a fat juicy worm dangling in front of him. Instantly, he is attracted by it. The word James uses is *enticed*. Like this little fish, we are all enticed from time to time. We see the bait, and it looks good. It will make us feel good. We want it.

Just as I put bait on a hook to lure fish in, so the Devil and the world put bait out there for us. But James says that we are enticed by our own natural desires, and we are lured toward the temptation, just as the fish is enticed by his hunger and lured toward the worm.

I read a story about a place off Cape Hatteras in North Carolina called Nags Head. There is a shallow, sandy area there called Diamond Shoals, where more than two thousand ships have wrecked. The story goes that two hundred years ago, men from Nags Head would take a horse and tie a bright lantern to its bridle. On dark, rainy nights, they would walk the horse up and down the shore, luring in ships that were looking for safety from the storm. The ships would be drawn in toward the light, and when they hit that shoal, they would be destroyed. Then the men would go down and plunder anything of value from them.

We are lured in because of our desires. Martin Luther said, "To fight against sin is to fight against the devil, the world, and one's self. The fight against one's self is the worst fight of all."[1]

## We Linger around the Bait

When we see that bait, of course we should immediately turn around and flee. Unfortunately, both humans and fish stay around too long.

When I see the little ball on my fishing pole bobbing around on the surface of the water, I know a fish is hanging around. He is playing with the bait. He is hungry, and he wants the worm, but he is not sure about it.

In her book *Secret Strength,* Joni Eareckson Tada writes about facing temptation. I used to think, "What would Joni know about temptation? She is paralyzed from the neck down." She tells of how she used to think she was entitled to slack off a little because of her disability. Then God changed her heart. She says, "When God allows you to suffer, do you have the tendency to use your very trials as an excuse for sinning? Or do you feel that since you've given God a little extra lately by taking such abuse, he owes you a day off?"[2]

Joni realized that she was being lured in by false thinking. She said that God doesn't give our morality a vacation. It is not okay to peacefully coexist with temptation in our lives.

In our family, when we go on a diet we always like to say, "There will be just one day a week when we can eat whatever we want." Do you ever do that? Pretty soon every day is that way, even though you start off with good intentions. God doesn't work like that, however. He doesn't say, "You can have one day a week to do whatever you want. You can be cruel, angry, or bitter. Sin as much as you like, because you've been stressed out, and you've been working hard." We may tell ourselves that's okay, but God has never approved it.

After the 1989 earthquake in Oakland and the Bay Area, there was a sharp increase in arrests for various crimes. People were under a lot of stress, so they turned to crime as a release from their situations. Temptation and stress were working together. As believers, we have to be especially careful of stressful times, because during those stressful times temptation can bombard us even more than usual.

## Once We Take the Bait, We Cannot Let Go

For me, it's a great feeling when I see that little bopper go under the water and feel a bit of tension on my fishing line. It means that I have hooked that fish, and he is not going anywhere.

Temptation is not a sin. Sin happens when we yield our wills to the temptation. That's when we get in trouble. The sin usually starts small, but when it grows big, it can destroy our lives. Our desires plus the external bait plus an act of the will gives birth to sin.

James says it this way in verse 15, "Then, after desire has conceived, it gives birth to sin; and sin, when it is full-grown, gives birth to death." Sin doesn't take twenty years to grow up as we humans do. It starts working against us the moment it is born.

If we do not spend time with God, developing our love relationship with him, how will we ever endure the temptation that comes before us? We need to balance our lives so that we have time for God, because without that relationship, we have no resistance to temptation. When a temptation comes along, it easily sparks a desire inside of us, and because we have no strength or ability to resist, we soon find ourselves defeated.

## We End Up in the Frying Pan

The moment you and I said yes to Jesus, we became an enemy of Satan. The Devil would like nothing more than to see us take the bait and end up sizzling in the frying pan of defeat.

German theologian Dietrich Bonhoeffer, author of *The Cost of Discipleship,* also wrote a short book called *Temptation.* In it he said, "In our members there is a slumbering inclination towards desire which is both sudden and fierce. With irresistible power, desire seizes mastery over the flesh. All at once a secret, smoldering fire is kindled. The flesh burns and is in flame."[3]

James says that when sin is born, it will give birth to death. Have you ever committed a sin and died? I have. After I have sinned, I have suddenly realized that there is no joy in my life. Everything looks different. I thought the sin was going to be okay, so I went for it. But afterward, I realized that it did not make me happy; in fact, it had just the opposite effect. I have had too many friends whose lives have been destroyed because they thought it was going to be okay to sin. They said, "Oh, the Lord understands that this is my weakness. It'll be fine." But they discovered too late that it wasn't fine. Yes, God understands our weaknesses, but he gives us the power to overcome them.

What is your temptation? Do you see how it is luring you in? What do you struggle with? Pride? Anger? Maybe it's a critical spirit. Or is it lying, laziness, or greed? What about the temptation to cheat in school, at work, or on your taxes? When you have thoughts like, "Go ahead, take that shortcut. Other people have done worse," are you able to resist the temptation? Or do you often end up in the frying pan?

When James penned these words, he didn't limit them to one particular sin. We may point our fingers at people and say, "Oh, their sin is worse than my sin." But James isn't addressing that issue here. James is saying that we all fall into temptations; we all yield our wills to things we know are wrong.

When we are able to see a temptation, recognize it, and release the power of the Holy Spirit to fight it, we are in pretty good shape. But if we get to the point in our lives where we see a specific sin and say, "Oh, that's just my one area of weakness," then we are in big trouble. Then that temptation has the power to destroy us. When it gives birth to sin, it will lead to death: physical death, death of a dream, death of a family, death of relationships, or death of our identity with God.

When the lure drops, and that little worm hangs there in front of our eyes, may we turn and run away, as Joseph did, saying, "No, thank you!" (see Genesis 39:1–12). Let's choose not to be a part of that kind of conversation, or not to be in those locations—whatever the temptation might be, let's run the other way. I pray that God will give you and me the strength to do that.

We know that our flesh is weak, but God's Spirit is strong. Only he can help us to gain victory over temptation.

## CHAPTER 6

# PRAISE GOD FROM WHOM ALL BLESSINGS FLOW

*JAMES 1:16–18*

Aseven-year-old boy cannot stop fidgeting during Sunday school. He tries to pay attention, but it is so hard to sit still. Finally, he can't take it any longer, and he yells out to the teacher, "Can we hurry up? This is so boring!"

A little girl turns quickly, punches him in the side, and says, "Be quiet. It's supposed to be boring."

One of my greatest fears when I am speaking is that people will think I am boring. I had some boring professors in college, and I have heard boring pastors at times. I don't want to be like them; I don't want to put people to sleep.

Are we bored with church and with God? Do we look at the world and think it looks like fun because God is so boring? Do we feel that God is mundane?

If so, James says to us, "Don't be deceived, my dear brothers. Every good and perfect gift is from above, coming down from the Father of the heavenly lights, who does not change like shifting shadows" (1:16–17).

Why are we bored with God? Because our hearts are distracted by the world. We need a better understanding of who God is. We need to know his character. Then we can praise the God from whom all blessings flow.

## God Is Not Out to Destroy Us

The word James uses for God in this passage is *Father* (1:17). In

Matthew 7:11, Jesus reminded us that even earthly fathers give good gifts to their children. How much more will our heavenly Father give us good gifts? Don't be deceived into thinking that somehow God is trying to trip you up and destroy you. He cares for you even more than an earthly father cares for his children.

I am worried sometimes by how easily I can be deceived. My mind plays tricks on me and tells me that something is okay when it's not. Someone once said, "The ingenuity of self-deception is inexhaustible." So James tells us not to be deceived. God is our Father, says James, and he is not trying to put sin in our way.

We cringe when we read stories in the newspaper of parents who have done horrible things to their kids. When we read a story about a mother who killed her own children, we groan inside and think, "How in the world could a parent do such a thing?"

When I think of my own kids, I can't imagine doing anything to cause them pain. But I have to remember that earthly fathers are not perfect. God, our heavenly Father, is perfect, and he does not want to see us in pain. James reminds us in the previous verses that God is not the one who tempts us. He does not seek to do us harm. On the contrary, he wants to bless us.

## God Is Benevolent

It is God's nature to give. In verse 17, James says, "Every good and perfect gift is from above." God does not give us temptations. He gives us good and perfect gifts, and we receive those gifts every day.

One of the most encouraging things we can do is look at our day and try to identify all the gifts God has given us in it. Instead of going through the day complaining and being negative, we should go through our day looking at all the wonderful gifts he has bestowed upon us. We need to understand that God is benevolent and that every day he gives us gifts. He gives us the gift of laughter. Today, we can laugh, we can smile, we can have joy. Health is a gift. Family is a gift. We are able to enjoy the gift of nature all around us. Because of God's goodness to us, we have the gifts of love, friendship, and forgiveness. Here James is telling us, "Listen, God is not giving you a temptation. No, God is the benevolent Father who is giving you good and perfect gifts."

As the psalmist said of God, "He makes me lie down in green pastures, he leads me beside quiet waters.... my cup overflows" (Psalm 23:2, 5). Every good and perfect gift—love, laughter, family, nature, joy, friends, church, everything that we have—has come down from the Father who says, "I want to bless you with a gift."

I always enjoy reading in the Old Testament about the way God dealt with Israel. Through his servant Moses, God told his people:

> See, I set before you today life and prosperity, death and destruction. For I command you today to love the LORD your God, to walk in his ways, and to keep his commands, decrees and laws; then you will live and increase, and the LORD your God will bless you in the land you are entering to possess.
>
> But if your heart turns away and you are not obedient, and if you are drawn away to bow down to other gods and worship them, I declare to you this day that you will certainly be destroyed. (Deuteronomy 30:15–18)

As we read that passage, we would think that the choice would be obvious. Who wouldn't want to choose life and blessing? God warned the Israelites of what would happen to them if they disobeyed him, but they disobeyed anyway. And still, again and again, he allowed them to repent, and he blessed them. What a picture of the benevolence of God. But what a picture of the way we act toward his benevolence.

I love the story of the prodigal son (see Luke 15:11–32). It is one of the greatest illustrations of God's love. Even though the son disobeyed and disrespected his father, when he finally returned, the father not only welcomed his son back, but he ran out to meet him. God our Father is waiting with open arms for us. He is running toward us, and he wants us to run to him.

When our kids are young, we like to pick them up, hug them, hold them, and kiss their chubby little cheeks. But do they want that? Of course not—they would rather be playing. I think God is the same way. He tries to hold on to us, but we get distracted by "fun stuff" that we think we would rather be doing. "Come on, spend some time with me," he says.

But we are full of excuses. "God, I've got so much to do today and so many people to meet. Maybe tonight ... or tomorrow." Our Father wants to be with us, but we have to make time for him.

Henri Nouwen said it best in his book, *The Return of the Prodigal Son.* "Here is the God I want to believe in: a Father who, from the beginning of creation, has stretched out his arms in merciful blessing, never forcing himself on anyone, but always waiting; never letting his arms drop down in despair, but always hoping that his children will return so that he can speak words of love to them ... his only desire is to bless."[1]

## God Does Not Change

In verse 17 James says that all our good and perfect gifts come from "the Father of the heavenly lights." The lights he is referring to are literally the heavenly bodies: the stars, the planets, and the sun that God created.

If our sun were hollow, it could hold 1.3 million Earths. That's a pretty big star. There is another star called Antares that could hold sixty-four million of our suns. Greater still is the star in the constellation of Hercules that could hold a hundred million stars the size of Antares.[2] Why did God create all this light? Because he is light, and he loves the light. We can look up at night and think, "Wow, God made those lights for *me*."

Revelation 21:23 describes heaven this way: "The city does not need the sun or the moon to shine on it, for the glory of God gives it light, and the Lamb is its lamp." As we walk through heaven, there won't be any shadows, because God's presence is light, and his presence will be everywhere.

Here in this passage, James is pointing out that God's character does not change. He doesn't have any shadows. He doesn't change like the seasons. God is the same yesterday, today, and forever (see Hebrews 13:8). In a world of uncertainties, we can have confidence in who God is: our heavenly Father, the Giver of good gifts, who does not change.

After my wife Deb and I got married, we enjoyed taking a few days off now and then to spend time with my college roommate, Terry, on his family's ranch. We kept up a great friendship with them over the years. The last time we went to visit, I was saddened that I did not recognize Terry's dad. At eighty-three years of age, after a stroke, a bout with cancer, and various operations, he was not the same. I remembered him bailing Terry out of all kinds of trouble during college, and now Terry was taking care of him. I was struck with the realization that all of us change. For one thing, we all grow older.

My wife is continually reminding me that I have changed. I am not the same person I was when I married her, she says. Our lives change, our families change, and our circumstances change. And yet, through all of that, God does not change. He is always the same. He is a benevolent Father who continues to give wonderful gifts to his beloved children.

Our Father showed his incredible love through the gift of his Son (see Romans 5:8). Why would he give us temptation when he has given us a new life in Christ?

There are churches across America that are filled with cultural Christians. I'm sure you have met some of them; I know I have. They like the pastor of the church, the people in the church, and the programs of the church. But even though they like church, something is still missing in their lives. Some of these people have said to me, "It's not real. I love the church, our pastor, and our friends. I love this place, but I don't know God, and I have never experienced him." Even church elders have come to me and confessed, "I don't know Jesus." People who have been in their church for fifty years have told me, "I just love the church, but I really don't know the Lord."

James has been asking us the question about our knowledge of Jesus Christ and our faith in him: Is it real? In verse 18 he says of God, "He chose to give us birth through the word of truth, that we might be a kind of firstfruits of all he created." God has given us a spiritual birth that has made us different people. St. Augustine wrote, "God has some that the church doesn't. The church has some that God doesn't."³ Only you and I know whether we have been born of the Spirit or not.

Have you been born again? Is it real to you? Here James is saying to you: "Don't be deceived. Don't think this temptation is coming from God because God has given you good and perfect gifts. And the greatest gift is his son, Jesus Christ, who brings you eternal life."

I don't know what is in your soul, but God does. Maybe you have gone through your life thinking, "This is good. I can go to church once a week, and everything will be fine." Do not base your security on church attendance. You need to base your security on the indwelling Christ, Jesus in you.

Right now, God is waiting for you to come to him. He is not out to destroy you; he wants to give you good gifts. He does not change, but he waits patiently for you to change. Have you surrendered your life to him? Is your faith real?

## CHAPTER 7

# GOD STILL SPEAKS— WE MUST LISTEN!

## JAMES 1:19–21

Several years ago, the vice chairman for the National Transportation Safety Board addressed a committee of frustrated flight attendants. They were upset by the lack of attention from airplane passengers during the mandatory routine safety demonstrations.

One flight attendant had even changed her standard line to add a little twist. She said, "When the oxygen mask drops down in front of you, place it over your navel and continue to breathe normally." No one even noticed.

I have certainly been among those inattentive passengers. Having flown many times, I have learned to tune out the instructions. I know what light leads to what light and where the exit doors are located.

Sometimes, however, the flight attendants really get my attention. One time I watched a woman turn every line of her routine into stand-up comedy. She really got into it, and pretty soon, everyone was laughing. At the end, we all clapped for her. People had listened to her. They had actually paid attention to what she was saying.

For many of us, listening can be a hard thing to do. We would rather talk most of the time. Listening takes some effort. In this passage, James is imploring us to listen.

## Quick to Listen

I would like to focus our attention on verse 19 where James says, "Be quick to listen, slow to speak and slow to become angry."

I am usually slow to listen, very quick to speak, and not so slow about getting angry. However, James, thinking back over the life of his half brother, Jesus, tells us, "No, we need to live the way Jesus lived his life."

For some people, listening is a real gift. You may be very good at listening. Others, like me, have to work hard at learning to listen.

One pastor was trying to explain to his congregation the difference between fact and faith. He said, "You are sitting before me ... that is a fact. I am standing in the pulpit ... that is a fact. I am speaking ... that is a fact. Whether you are actually listening to me ... that is faith."

Hearing is easy, but listening is much more difficult. Sometimes we think people are good listeners because they seem to stare at us very intently while we are speaking, but in reality their mind is skiing, or on a motorcycle ride, or planting flowers in the garden. It takes real effort to actually listen.

James is telling us to listen. Listen to whom? Listen to God. Why is that so important? Because it is at the core of our relationship with him. He sent his Son to die for us, and he wants to have communication and fellowship with us. If God didn't want anything to do with us, why should we follow him? We may as well worship a rock or a crystal.

God does talk to us. The question is: Do we listen?

God speaks to us through his Word, and he uses the Holy Spirit to prompt our hearts to do something in response to it. In John 8:47 Jesus said to some of the people of his day, "He who belongs to God hears what God says. The reason you do not hear is that you do not belong to God." Later, in chapter 10, Jesus tells us that we know God's voice the way sheep know their shepherd's voice. If we cannot hear his voice, if we do not recognize or understand it, if we are not quick to listen to his leading, something is wrong with our relationship.

God saved us so that we could hear him. The Spirit of God dwells in us so that we can listen to his voice. He speaks to us and he leads us through his Word. One of my favorite authors, François Fenelon, wrote, "God never ceases to speak to us, but the noise of the world without and the tumult of our passions within bewilder us and prevent us from listening to him."[1]

I used to read the stories of great Christian missionaries who heard God's voice tell them to do something, and when they did it, miracles happened. I would get discouraged by these stories and become dissatisfied with my Christian life because what I was reading and what I was experiencing were two different things. I thought, "Surely, God, if those men and women heard your voice and acted in obedience to it, then I should be able to do so as well. God, teach me to hear and know your voice."

For a long time, I continued to pray, "God, let me hear your voice. Let me know, understand, and recognize it." At the same time, I was studying and meditating on God's Word and cultivating my relationship with him.

One day I came home, and Deb was standing at the front door with a disgusted look on her face. The washing machine had broken, and she knew that I was not Mr. Fix-It. "Let's go down to the laundromat," she said.

When we arrived and walked in, I saw a man with dirty clothing and messy hair looking through the trashcans for something to eat. All of a sudden I heard this small voice say to me, "Dan, buy him dinner."

"Lord, I've been wanting to hear your voice, but I'm not sure this is it," I thought.

Again, I felt that prodding. "Dan, buy him dinner."

I began to negotiate with God. "Okay, if he's still here when Deb's done with the laundry, I'll go take care of him."

He was sitting on a bench in the back of the laundromat when Deb finished and turned to leave. I sighed, walked over, and offered to buy him something to eat. He accepted, so I went next door and got him a hamburger, french fries, and root beer as he requested. I gave him the food and some money, then Deb and I got in the car and left. I never talked to him about Jesus, never said a word about God. I just kept hearing the Lord tell me to buy him dinner, so I did.

Six months later, I was in Portland, Oregon, to preach at a rescue mission. I didn't know anyone there, but as I finished my talk, I spotted someone who looked vaguely familiar. It was the man I had bought a meal for—six months earlier and six hundred miles away. I was able to meet him again, and that night I gave him more than a hamburger. He got the Word of God.

## Listening to God

The Spirit of God does speak to us. But we have to be willing to listen. God wants to encourage us, he wants to lead us, and he wants to empower our lives. So how do we listen?

First, we study the Bible. Some people are confused by the word *study*. I am not talking about simply reading *The Daily Bread* or some other daily devotional. If we go to church, Sunday school, and a Bible study during the week, that is all great, but that is not what I mean when I say, "Study the Bible." We need time alone with God and his Word. This leads into the next step: meditation.

Psalm 1:2 says of the man who is blessed by God, "His delight is in the law of the LORD, and on his law he meditates day and night." Meditating on God's Word does not involve "emptying the mind" as some of the Eastern religions define it. Meditation means filling our minds with the Word of God, then pondering it, reflecting on it, and considering how it might pertain to us. After we have read a passage thoroughly and studied it carefully, then it is time to chew on it for a while.

Most of us don't have time for meditation. We just have time to grab the Bible, flip it open to a random passage, read a few verses, and call it quits. We may think briefly about how what we have just read might apply to our lives or how we can use it to teach our Sunday school classes, but we don't allow it to penetrate our minds, wills, and emotions. If we read the Bible without allowing it to have an impact on us, if it does not change us from the inside out, then we have missed the whole point.

The purpose of reading the Bible is not so much to gain knowledge as it is to transform our lives. Meditation causes us to think: "God, that's me. I need to change. I need you to work on something inside of me."

The third step involves moving from meditation to contemplation. Contemplation goes further and deeper than meditation. Webster's dictionary defines the word *contemplate* as "to view or consider with continued attention," and the word *contemplation* as "a state of mystical awareness of God's being."[2] We move from reflecting on the passage we have just read to contemplating the nature and being of God. We are not rushed, we don't say much; we just dwell on the majesty, greatness, and awesomeness of God.

Joyce Huggett, in her book *The Joy of Listening to God*, said of this process: "We bask in the warmth of his love. We feel his gaze on us. He fills us afresh with his spirit. We receive a new perspective on life—his perspective. We draw so close to his heart that we sense his concern for the world and from our contemplation flows intercession as we catch his compassion for the hurting world."[3]

I encourage you to study the Bible not only to gain knowledge but also to develop an ear that listens for God to speak. Do you have times when you think the Lord may be speaking to you to do something, but you aren't sure? I encourage you to do it anyway. See what happens. You may be very surprised. Be open to God's prompting.

Have you ever done a random act of kindness for someone who later told you, "That was just what I needed. How did you know?" (I love it when that happens.) You may not have even realized it, but you heard God's voice, and he used you to meet the needs of someone else.

Contemplation can take a bit of time. If you are retired, you probably have a lot of time. If you are semi-retired, you probably have much time. If you have a full-time job and a family to care for, you have some time. If you are a single mother of three children under the age of five, you have no time and no life. But no matter what your circumstance is, no matter what stage of life you are in right now, decide when you are going to make time for study, meditation, and contemplation.

The wonderful part is that you can meditate and contemplate while changing diapers, mowing the lawn, or sitting in traffic. Meditation is a matter of the heart. Sometimes it is good to find a quiet, relaxing place, but that is not always possible. Just be quick to listen when you study, meditate, and contemplate.

## Slow to Speak and Become Angry

Someone has said, "We need to keep our words soft and sweet because we never know when we're going to have to eat them."

A Jewish folk saying goes, "Men have two ears but one tongue, that we should hear more than we speak. The ears are always open, ever ready to receive instruction, but the tongue is surrounded with a double row of teeth to hedge it in and keep it within proper balance."

We are often too quick to speak. We don't take enough time to think about the impact of our words. Sometimes this happens because we are too quick to become angry. This anger comes from the selfish thought, "I am not being heard."

Winston Churchill said, "A man is as big as the things that make him angry."[4] Benjamin Franklin said, "Whatever is begun in anger ends in shame."[5] But God says it best, as always, in Proverbs 14:17: "A quick-tempered man does foolish things."

How do we become slow to speak? How do we control our anger? By studying, by listening, by meditating, by contemplating.

The greatest opportunity we have is to stop, meditate, and contemplate on the forgiveness that is ours in Jesus Christ. That is the greatest gift we have. We are forgiven. God sees us through his son Jesus, and therefore we can stand clean before him.

I challenge you. Don't just read the Bible. Don't just study the Bible. Meditate on the Bible. Let God's Word speak to you. We meditate on life, on retirement, and on investments. We all replay pleasant scenes a thousand times in our heads. You know how to meditate. Why not meditate on God's Word?

Is it real? Is your faith real? Is it real enough for you to know the voice of God? Is it real enough for you to experience that change in your heart that keeps you from speaking more quickly than you should and becoming angry when you should not?

## CHAPTER 8

# JUST DO IT!

*JAMES 1:22–25*

For many years, our family lived about three miles from Nike World Headquarters in Portland, Oregon. One of the great legends of Portland is a man named Phil Knight, who, many years ago, discovered how to make a better type of running shoe by using a waffle iron on the soles. He started selling these shoes out of the trunk of his car. Today, he is known as the founder of Nike Corporation, a four-billion-dollar company.

I read a story in the *Oregonian* newspaper that told about a time when Nike was attempting to figure out its next ad campaign. Several high-powered advertising companies came up with ideas, but none of them satisfied Mr. Knight. Everyone was getting discouraged.

A few days later, a senior executive was walking through Nike and heard an employee giving orders to other employees. "Just do it!" he said. The phrase had been popular around Nike, and often when someone complained about a job, they were told, "Just do it." This executive thought about it for a while, then went to Mr. Knight with his idea. That phrase became one of the premier advertising campaigns the world has ever seen.

James has some strong words for us in these verses. In today's world he might have said, "Just do it." The person who looks into the Word of God and is not changed is like a man who sees himself in the mirror one morning, disheveled and dirty, yet just ignores his appearance. But the person who looks into the Word, and does what it says, is blessed.

This passage is truly about obedience—and disobedience. James is concerned about and frustrated with these Christians. He is saying to them, "Just do it. Don't reason. Don't argue. Don't make excuses. Just do it." He wants them—and us—to be doers of the Word, not just hearers.

## Disobedience Is Rooted in Self-Deception

Too many times, we view church as a spectator sport. We come in and sit down, we listen to the music and enjoy the pastor's jokes, but we don't really enter into the service. We can sit week after week listening to sermons, but never be involved in actually doing what we hear.

Wales has produced some very famous preachers through the years. During my first trip there, I had the opportunity to speak at an old church in the pulpit of Martin Lloyd Jones. I also spoke at the church where Evan Roberts started the Welsh revival, which had a great impact on America. These visits were incredibly moving experiences for me.

While I was there, I learned the value of the Welsh sermons. The people I met value oratory skills and the gift of presentation. They especially love sermons, Christian or non-Christian. However, they don't listen to the sermons to be changed. When I finished speaking, they would say, "That was a great sermon," but they had no intention of heeding it, because to them the sermon was all about the presentation.

In verse 22, James says, "Do not merely listen to the word, and so deceive yourselves. Do what it says." In this verse, the word *do* indicates a continuous action. Doing what Jesus commanded should be a part of our lifestyles. I think James had in mind the people whom Jesus spoke of in Matthew 7:21–23. They thought they were Christians, but Jesus told them, "I never knew you." A true disciple learns so he can do—not just so he can teach others.

I have many friends who want to be Bible teachers. Some have told me that they have the gift of teaching. One friend quit his job to become a teacher. Unfortunately, I have seen some teachers who should not be teaching.

These people are more interested in how teaching makes them feel. They enjoy being in front of people. They enjoy that sense of power—"You sit, and I'll talk to you and impart my wonderful knowledge to you." It makes them feel important. It makes them feel special and needed. Unfortunately, they rarely live what they teach.

I am a little leery of teaching. I have discovered that I would rather be an evangelist than a pastor any day of the week. As an evangelist, I can use most of my material again, and some of it I get to use many times. If I am going to speak to children, I go to my files and pull out a children's message. If I am going to be speaking to business professionals, I pull out a message tailored to them. The gospel story really doesn't change that much.

Now, as a pastor, I have learned that I need new material every week. I have also discovered that I can't just teach it; I have to live it. It's one thing to say, "I found this in the Bible, and I thought I'd tell you about it"; it's quite another thing to live out what is being taught. When people tell me that they want to be a teacher, they often don't realize that it comes with a great responsibility (see James 3:1–2).

James is telling these Christians, "Don't just study the Word. Don't just look at it. Learn it, know it, understand it, and pass that information along to someone else. But don't forget: The reason you study and meditate on God's Word is to live it."

C. S. Lewis said, "I was not born to be free. I was born to adore and to obey."[1] Think carefully about that statement. We were born to adore, to worship, to lift our hands to the Lord and say: "God, I love you. You are forever with me. I adore you. I worship you. God, I want to obey you. I'm going to do what you ask me to do."

What does it mean to be a doer of the Word? James is not just talking about teaching children's church or serving on a committee or leading music on Sunday mornings. He is talking about being obedient to whatever God tells us to do.

Jesus has given us certain commandments. These are not suggestions for us to consider if we feel like it, but things for us to do whether we feel like it or not. In John 13:34–35, he tells us: "A new command I give you: Love one another. As I have loved you, so you must love one another. By this all men will know that you are my disciples, if you love one another." Also, in Luke 6:31, he says, "Do to others as you would have them do to you."

As I look at these and other commands of Jesus, I ask myself, "Am I a doer of the Word?" I answer myself, "Of course you are. You're a pastor, you counsel people, you have an evangelistic ministry. Absolutely, you are a doer."

However, Jesus reminds me, "Yes, you're doing all those wonderful things, Dan, but are you really doing what I've asked you to do?" James doesn't want us to be deceived into thinking that we are obeying the Lord merely because we appear to be good Christians. True followers of Jesus obey *all* his commands.

When I meditate and contemplate on Scripture, these questions come to mind: "Do I really love Jesus? Am I really a doer of the Word? Do I live out my faith, not just at church on Sundays, but every day of the week? Do I treat others the way I want them to treat me? Do I judge others? Is my obedience showing that I truly love Jesus?"

## Disobedience Causes Us to Forget

The words *looks* and *looking* in verses 23 and 24 are forms of the word *look*, which in this context means "to glance, to look at quickly." This person walks by the mirror, glances at it, then walks away and forgets what he saw. As you head out the door in the morning, perhaps you take a quick glance in the mirror to make sure your tie is straight, or your makeup looks nice. Some people do that with God's Word. They take a quick glance at it and say "I'm all right." Even though they read the words, they have no intention of obeying them.

A fortune-teller was studying the hand of a young man. "You will be poor and very unhappy until you are thirty-seven years old," she said solemnly.

The young man was a little concerned. "Then what?" he asked. "Will I be rich and happy after that?"

"No, you'll still be poor," the fortune-teller replied, "but by then you'll be used to it."

That's kind of the way we listen to the Word of God. We hear the same stories. We hear the same passages of Scripture, and we just get used to it. Then we become careless listeners. We take a quick glance at God's Word, but we forget what we are supposed to be doing. Some people use the phrase, "It's like riding a bicycle," indicating that once we have learned a skill, we never lose it. However, that is not always true.

I was having lunch with a friend of mine who is the assistant district attorney for the city of San Diego. Dan is a great Christian man, a great leader, and a great police officer. He told me the whole story of how he got into police work. He shared about the time when he transitioned from being behind a desk to being back on the street. His comment was, "It is a very frightening thing to be put back on the street after a long period of time working in the station. You have all the knowledge, and all the training, but you haven't used it for a while. You feel very vulnerable because your reaction time has slowed." If we don't use our reading and listening skills, we start to lose them; we begin to forget.

Jesus gives us commands like "Love one another" (John 13:34), "Do to others as you would have them do to you" (Luke 6:31), and "First take the plank out of your own eye, and then you will see clearly to remove the speck from your brother's eye" (Matthew 7:5). But when we don't obey these commands, we forget what we are supposed to be doing.

Could it be that we are only glancing at Jesus and his words? Could it be that we really have no intention of obeying them? Could it be that we want Jesus as Savior, but not as Lord?

A cathedral in Lübeck, Germany, has a famous inscription on its wall attributed to St. Germain. Paraphrased, it says:

> You call me Master and obey me not. You call me Light and see me not. You call me the Way and walk with me not. You call me Wise and follow me not. You call me Fair and love me not. You call me Rich and ask me not. You call me Eternal and seek me not. You call me Gracious and trust me not. You call me Noble and serve me not.

You call me Mighty and honor me not. You call me Just
and fear me not. If I condemn you, blame me not.[2]

As I read that inscription, I thought, "Lord, am I a doer of your
Word? Or have I been deceiving myself? Have I only glanced at
your Word and quickly forgotten what I'm supposed to be doing?"

We can say that we love God and that we are walking with him,
but if we continue day after day and month after month without
living out his commandments, then we are not true followers and
disciples.

True joy comes when we say, "Lord, I want to be a doer of your
Word. I want to be obedient to what you've told me to do." Being the
people that God wants us to be will bring true joy and contentment.

## CHAPTER 9

# GIVE ME THAT OLD-TIME RELIGION

## JAMES 1:26–27

We often prefer the old to the new. Old shoes are more comfortable than new shoes. New things are unfamiliar and confusing. Some of the Eastern European countries that have recently gained freedom and democracy find their new governments very confusing. If given a choice between democracy and Communism, some probably would choose Communism simply because that is what they know.

We like the old—the old way of doing things, the old way of saying things. We long for the "good ol' days." We long for the days of the Cold War when we knew who our enemies were instead of this new day of terrorism in which we can't see them and don't know where they are coming from.

The old gospel song says, "Give me that old-time religion; it's good enough for me." I think if James were writing today he would talk to us about that "old-time religion." Seemingly it was good enough for the composer of this song, good enough for past generations. But what is that old-time religion? Is it ceremony? Is it law? Is it going through the motions? What actually is this "old-time religion"?

I like the way the *Living Bible* puts these verses: "Anyone who says he is a Christian but doesn't control his sharp tongue is just fooling himself, and his religion isn't worth much. The Christian who is pure and without fault, from God the Father's point of view, is the one who takes care of orphans and widows, and who remains true to the Lord—not soiled and dirtied by his contacts with the world" (James 1:26–27).

In this passage, James is asking, "What is religion? What is this relationship with God supposed to be about?"

Karl Marx said, "Man makes religion. Religion does not make man."[1] James is concerned because ceremony has become so important to the church that it is overlooking the basics. Because the church is emphasizing the formal procedures of worship, the service is not touching people's hearts.

Blaise Pascal, the French physicist, said, "Men never do evil so completely and cheerfully as when they do it from religious conviction."[2] We can see that fact in history, and we can see it in our modern day. If people are doing something in the name of religion, they think it can't possibly be wrong.

So what is true religion? What is a true relationship with God? How do we know whether our faith is real?

## By Our Speech

In verse 26 James says, "If anyone considers himself religious and yet does not keep a tight rein on his tongue, he deceives himself and his religion is worthless." If we say that we are followers of Jesus, and that we truly have him in our hearts, how can we use our tongues to create all kinds of pain and hurt and to stir up fights? James saw that what the believers of his day had learned and what they were living did not agree.

In this verse James is referring to those who are not exerting control over their speech. He is not specific about what is going on, but he knows that what is coming from these people's mouths is what is in their hearts. We can deceive people by acting pious, by getting all dressed up, going to church and singing, but what comes out of our mouths, the words we say when we think no one is looking, reveal our true colors. Words are like a window to the soul.

James tells us that if we can't control our tongues, our religion is basically worthless. This truth can apply to words that are written as well as spoken. An unkind e-mail or a hateful letter shows where the heart is just as much as a harsh word or a hurtful remark.

One of the greatest weaknesses of believers today is in the area of speech. Words communicate our feelings, they reveal who we are, and they come from our hearts. They often do great damage. We would probably never put the sins of speech in a category with immorality or any of the other grave sins, but James is very clear here. If we say we are Christians, and our words do not prove it, our religion is a waste of time.

## By Our Service

How does this old-time religion affect our service? A true and sincere experience with God will penetrate us with life-changing force. We will become benevolent. James is telling us that if we are truly religious, we will have an attitude of service. He gives the example of looking after orphans and widows.

Now this does not mean that we just need to set up an orphanage or a home for widows. That is not the spirit of what he is saying. James is talking about an attitude of benevolence toward those who are truly helpless. At the time he was writing, orphans and widows had no one to take care of them. There was no Social Security, no universal health care, no government housing. People in need had to rely entirely on the kindness and assistance of their friends and families to survive.

In the country of Moldova, where I have done some evangelistic work, the economic system is a mess. The average person makes the equivalent of about fifty dollars a month. One of the goals of the church there is to open up an orphanage. Why? Because the government cannot, or will not, take care of orphaned kids. A pastor in Moldova started a church that went from zero to a thousand members in seven years. These people definitely have evangelistic zeal, and a desire to reach their community.

In America, we have churches that start preschools to help the needs of our society. Working moms need a place to put their children. The church wants to have a Christian impact on those young kids' lives, so it starts a preschool. That is what James is talking about. Reaching out to those who need to hear the gospel, and taking care of them, not only spiritually, but also physically, mentally, and emotionally.

James is saying to us today, "Okay, you say you're a follower of Jesus. Let's see what is coming out of your mouth and what is in your heart. What are your actions saying about you? Are you showing benevolence to those who need it, and giving help to those who are helpless?"

I know of churches that have a true spirit of benevolence. They care for their members in many ways. Some set up a special fund to give financial assistance to families in emergency situations. Others put together a meal service to bring aid to new mothers, people recovering from surgery, or those in the midst of tragedy. In God's sight, these people are practicing a pure and faultless religion.

## By Our Separation

In verse 27 James sets forth the third aspect of true religion: "to keep oneself from being polluted by the world." That's a tricky one. It doesn't mean that we can't enjoy living in the world. Some church people haven't smiled for forty years because they think Christians aren't supposed to enjoy life in this world. I don't see that principle demonstrated in the life of Jesus. He enjoyed life. He enjoyed social gatherings and being with people. And enjoyment of life is not limited to the New Testament. The Old Testament talks frequently about people getting together and having parties that lasted for days. In Old Testament times as well as in New Testament days, godly life was about joy.

We certainly can enjoy life. Separation from the world has to do with our attitudes, what's in our hearts, and what's important to us. Everything we enjoy in this world has to come second to our purpose in Christ.

When I came to the Lord, I was told, "Good Christians don't go to movies. Movies support Hollywood." True, the money spent on movie tickets helps pay for the actors and actresses and all the questionable things many of them do on and off the screen. However, I have a problem when someone says, "You went to a movie? I'll be praying for you." Yet, without a second thought, that same person will attend a baseball game, supporting many athletes who are known to be anti-God. At ball games, they listen to foul language and are exposed to fans drinking excessive amounts of beer.

That is not the real issue. Jesus didn't say, "Get out of the world and never have any contact with it." Even though God hates the sin in the world, he still loves the world, and he sent his Son to die for it. He told us to be lights in the world (see Matthew 5:14). If we don't have any interaction with the world, we can't have any godly influence on it.

It is a real tragedy that many Christians choose not to deal with unbelievers unless they absolutely must do so. Rather than avoiding all contact with unbelievers, we should be building relationships that give us opportunities to witness to them. In some cases, that may mean going to the movies or attending a ball game to begin to build a relationship.

The average person in the United States probably lives about seventy-seven years.[3] Why? Just what are we supposed to accomplish during those seventy-seven years? We are not here by accident. We were designed, created, and put on planet Earth for a purpose. What is our purpose? If it is just to accumulate wealth, just to become famous or to have power, or even just to survive, then what good is it going to do us? We can't take it with us when we die.

What does God want us to do? Who does God want us to be? God could have designed this process so that we would immediately be taken to heaven when we accepted him. But he didn't. He left us here in the world because he has a purpose for us. What is it?

We often tell each other glibly, "God has a plan for your life." Unfortunately, many of those who say that are not really convinced of it. I believe that God does have a plan for each of our lives. God has something for each one of us to do. Have we discovered it? Are we doing it? Are we being the people God wants us to become?

Albert Schweitzer was a theology professor with a great ministry who decided to establish a medical mission in Africa. When asked why he became a medical doctor, he said, "For years I had been giving myself out in words and it was with joy that I followed the calling of a theological teacher and preacher.... This new form of activity [medicine] I could not represent to myself as talking about the religion of love, but only as an actual putting it into practice."[4] That is a purpose.

James wants us to be careful about the world, because our primary mission here is to be dispensers of God's love to people. We are supposed to shine forth, to be light, and to lift up God to others. In order to be that witness, we must shine forth into the darkness, while being careful not to let the darkness consume us. Jesus asked the Father for us, "My prayer is not that you take them out of the world but that you protect them from the evil one" (John 17:15).

Whether we are at work or at home, in the office or on the road, taking care of a family or struggling through college, God has a specific individual purpose for our lives. He also has one purpose that applies to all of us: to shine forth his love to others, whether it's our families, friends, neighbors, or coworkers.

I have a long way to go in that area. I think most of us do; the important thing is that we are moving in the right direction. Let's get back to that old-time religion—taking care of people and sharing Christ with them.

Is it real? Only you know the answer to that question. Your speech, your spirit of service, and your attitude toward the world all tell something about your faith, but only you and God know what's really in your heart. Continue to evaluate your faith, look deep inside your heart, and say, "Lord, am I the person you want me to be?"

## CHAPTER 10

# THESE ARE A FEW OF MY FAVORITE THINGS—AND PEOPLE

## JAMES 2:1–11

A young man is proposing to his girlfriend as they sit overlooking a lake. "I just want you to know how special you are to me," he begins. "I know I'm not wealthy, and I don't have a mansion, a yacht, and a Rolls Royce like Johnny Green. But I love you, and I want to marry you."

His girlfriend thinks a moment before responding. "I love you too, with all of my heart ... but could you tell me a little more about this Johnny Green?"

Even though we may love people for who they are, it is often easier to love those with a lot of money or possessions. We have a few of our favorite things, and our favorite people, and we are drawn to those people who have what we want.

As we look at James' life and personality, we begin to realize that this man has great emotion. When I picture him reading this passage out loud, it isn't in a monotone voice. It is with a booming, powerful voice, emphasizing the key parts with fervency and pastoral passion.

"My brothers, as *believers* in our *glorious* Lord Jesus Christ, *don't* show favoritism" (James 2:1).

This word *favoritism* that James uses here literally means "receiving the face," or making a judgment based on the external appearance of a person. Favoritism is often based on qualities like physical appearance, social status, and race. It is an attitude that is expected in the world, but one that James says should not be evidenced in true followers of Jesus Christ.

James begins with an imperative in verse 5, *Listen!* He is trying to wake up his readers. He wants them to really hear what he is trying to say to them.

James asks his readers why they are insulting the poor and showing favoritism to the rich. The rich nobles are the ones who are exploiting them and taking them to court! Why are his readers giving preference to the very people who are abusing them?

## Favoritism Is Selfish

It is important to note that the early believers were very poor, both economically and socially. They were farmers and craftsmen, not merchants or nobles of the day.

If you travel around the world, you will notice that many poor cultures have an incredible openness toward the gospel. I observed this phenomenon when I was in Moldova, one of the poorest countries in all of Europe. When I preached the good news there, the people responded very emotionally, and many of them came to know Jesus as Savior. They had a hunger to hear about him.

A few weeks later, I was in Poland, a much more modern country. The citizens of that nation have big shopping centers, grocery stores, and a McDonald's on almost every corner, just as we Americans do. It is a completely different culture and society from Moldova. When it comes to Jesus and responding to the gospel, the people of Poland are not nearly as receptive as those of the poorer country.

That doesn't mean, however, that just because someone is poor, he must be a Christian, or that because someone is wealthy, she must be a non-Christian. But for the most part, the poor are much more open to spiritual things.

As I look at American culture, I sometimes wonder: If we were poor, would we still follow Jesus? The poverty of some cultures makes it easier for people to follow Jesus. In other societies, materialism makes it easier to follow him. In America, it is easy for us to say that we are Christians when nothing bad is happening to us. No one is waiting to drag us off to be burned at the stake. We can say that we are Christians and still enjoy all the good things of life.

When I was in Moldova, I spoke with a lady named Olga. In her broken English, she talked about her life under Communist rule. "When the Communists persecuted us, the church was on fire, and Christians were on fire," she said. "We lived to serve. All we cared about was somebody coming to Jesus." I asked her what had changed. "Oh, now it is terrible," she said. "We have so much, so many things; everybody just cares about what they have."

Similarly, the early Christians to whom James is writing have forgotten their purpose. Instead of winning as many as possible for the kingdom, they are selfishly concerned with showing favoritism to the rich, hoping that they can gain some advantage from it.

James reminds his readers that the rich are the ones exploiting them and dragging them into court. Obviously, they know that they are being abused; but they are showing favoritism to these wealthy people because they hope to receive some benefit from them. They think that if they make a concession by saying, "Come here; sit in the good seat," they will get something out of the deal.

James also wants to show these Christians the benefit of being poor—they have no ties to the present world. Thus, in many ways, it is much easier to be tied to the next world. Their attitude should be: "This is not my home; I'm just passing through. What can you do to me? I don't have a big house or lots of money for you to take from me. All you can take is my life, and if you take that, I will be better off anyway." James is pointing out to them that they are poor materialistically but rich spiritually—rich in the kingdom to come (2:5). He wants them to see that they don't need the world's wealth to make them happy.

## Favoritism Is Deceitful

James is upset because these Christians are showing favoritism to the same people who are exploiting and abusing them. The word *exploiting* in verse 6 carries the connotation of a very hostile and brutal way of literally depriving people of their rights. Even though their basic rights are being taken away, they are still lifting

up the rich in front of everyone. They are being deceitful, not only
to these rich people, but also to themselves.

James reminds them that their importance does not come
from being with important people. They should not give preferential treatment to anyone, no matter how wealthy and powerful
they are.

I have been at several events where a famous person has walked
into the room—a politician, a musician, an actor—and the crowd
goes wild. The people's personalities changed because they were
with someone who made them feel more important.

One day I was sitting, reading a book in a Red Carpet Club
room at O'Hare Airport in Chicago. Suddenly I noticed a commo-
tion out of the corner of my eye; I looked up to see actor Danny
Glover sitting two seats down from me. A flood of people had surrounded him to ask for his autograph. I was amazed at how quickly
the personalities in the room had changed.

Unfortunately, people in a situation of importance often use it
to their advantage. In our society, we have special interest groups
who go to Washington and flash their money to get what they
want. Through my discussions with a variety of pastors over the
years, I have begun to understand that our churches are often run
the same way. We have special interest groups who take their area
of concern and begin to change things to suit themselves through
use of their money and personalities. Sadly, there are many stories
of churches that have been destroyed by such special interest
groups and their self-serving activities.

I have a friend who was being wooed to pastor a church that he
wasn't quite sure about. Finally, the church offered him fifty thousand dollars to renovate his office at the church, so he took the job.
He now has a beautifully renovated office, but he is not happy.

People come to church expecting to find a place to belong, a
place to worship and serve, but instead what they often find is a
house of special interest groups and church politics. James is very
concerned about this kind of thing happening to the early church.
He wants to remind them that showing favoritism to those with
money and influence is deceitful.

## Favoritism Is Disobedient

The Bible could not be clearer in this passage. James says that if we show favoritism—whether it is within the church or outside of it—then we are sinning:

> If you really keep the royal law found in Scripture, "Love your neighbor as yourself," you are doing right. But if you show favoritism, you sin and are convicted by the law as lawbreakers. For whoever keeps the whole law and yet stumbles at just one point is guilty of breaking all of it. (James 2:8–10)

On my trip to Poland, I had the opportunity to visit the Nazi concentration camp at Auschwitz. Here the Germans held their prisoners of war, as well as gypsies, homosexuals, Jews, and anyone else they considered inferior or who did not agree with their beliefs. These men, women, and children were either worked or starved to death (or were murdered outright).

I will never forget that experience. As we entered the gas chambers, people wept openly at the sight. In one corner was a stack of twenty thousand shoes representing a small portion of the 1.1 million people who had been exterminated in the chamber.

As I walked through Auschwitz, I was not thinking, "How in the world could the Germans do this?" What kept coming to my mind was, "How could we do this? How could God's creation, human beings, do something so horrible to their fellow humans?" Favoritism says, "Let's get rid of these people. They don't look like us, they don't talk like us, and they don't believe the way we do, so let's just get rid of them." This event was a monumental experience of understanding how ugly human nature can be.

What is our intention? Is it to be with important people? Or is it to be a people of love? Is it to be noticed by others? Or is it to be people who accept others who may not look, think, dress, and act just the way we do?

When the teachers of the law asked Jesus what the greatest commandment was, he answered:

"Love the Lord your God with all your heart and with all
your soul and with all your mind and with all your
strength." The second is this: "Love your neighbor as
yourself." There is no commandment greater than these.
(Mark 12:30–31)

In our society, love is mocked, kindness cursed, and mercy
ridiculed. Power is everything. In our churches, we are not immune
to that worldly mind-set. Power offers an easy substitute for the
hard task of love. It is easier to be god than to love God; it is easier
to control people than to love people.

As I look at my own life, and as I think about Auschwitz and
about this passage from James, I ask myself, "Do I love the way
Jesus loves?" The gospels are full of stories about Jesus interact-
ing with people of all kinds. I am frustrated when I look at my
heart and my life. I must confess, "No, I don't love like that. Not
all the time."

Where is love? Does it reign supreme in our lives, or do we show
favoritism? Do we treat everyone with respect, or do we have a few
of our favorites to whom we show partiality? We need to ask God to
turn our selfish, deceitful, disobedient hearts into  hearts of love,
mercy, and compassion that see other people the way he sees them.

## CHAPTER 11

# OH MERCY, MERCY ME

## JAMES 2:12–13

After a worship service, an elderly woman stops to talk to the new pastor, who has only been there a few months. "I'm nearly deaf, and I can't really hear your message, but I still like to be here in church," she informs him.

The pastor, trying to make her feel better, replies, "Don't worry about that; you're not really missing much anyway."

"I know," she says, "that's what everyone's been telling me."

The woman probably could have shown a little more mercy toward the poor man. For some of us, mercy comes easily; for others, it does not. This story represents a subject that we all need to think more about—mercy.

## Our Mercy Will Be Revealed before God

In James 2:1–11, he deals with showing favoritism and partiality to individuals. In verses 12–13, James is talking about the royal law of love, and how it should move and motivate us in life. In verse 12 he says, "Speak and act as those who are going to be judged by the law that gives freedom."

James is telling us here that we will be held accountable for the mercy that we show—or do not show. The New International Version doesn't give the full strength of the words "speak and act." The literal translation is "so speak and so act," and is an imperative. It has a sense of urgency. Showing mercy is a display of love, and should happen on a regular basis. It should be a way of life. We need to look at our lives and say, "Is my faith real? Am I showing love and mercy to other people?"

Then James brings in the idea of God's judgment. This is not based on the pharisaical laws of legalism, but on the law of love. We will all stand before God and be judged by him.

People have always made fun of preachers for their "hellfire and damnation" messages. There is no doubt that some pastors have abused this idea of God's judgment through the years and used it as a way to manipulate people through fear and guilt. However, it is still an intense thought to consider that we will one day stand before God and give an account of our lives. It is certainly a cause for reflection and self-examination.

Jonathan Edwards, the great theologian of the 1700s who led a time of great revival in America, penned a little sermon called "Sinners in the Hands of an Angry God." Edwards would get up to preach on Sunday nights, slump over the podium slightly, and read his sermons, not even looking at his audience.

As he read this sermon, one line stood out as he communicated God's rightful wrath in sentencing people to hell: "You hang by a slender thread, with the flames of divine wrath flashing about it, and ready every moment to singe it, and burn it asunder."[1] By the time he was done, people would be literally clinging to the posts of the church, fearing for their lives. They realized that if they died, they would have to stand before God in judgment. It was a powerful message.

Today, we go to the other extreme. We don't want to hear about judgment at all, so we make the Christian life seem like a walk in the park. We tell people that Jesus will be with them and bless them, and they will be happy and joyful all the time.

I wish we could have a more balanced approach toward this area of judgment. Unfortunately, we go for months without even thinking about the fact that we will stand before the Lord and give an account to him of our lives. We live carelessly in many ways because we are not acutely aware of our impending judgment.

In 2 Corinthians 5:10, Paul wrote, "For we must all appear

before the judgment seat of Christ, that each one may receive what is due him for the things done while in the body, whether good or bad." Notice that he used the word *all*. Attendance is mandatory. You will be there. I will be there. Everyone will be there. The word *appear* means to show openly—as in a public trial—so that everything is known.

For those of us who have said yes to Jesus, we are not going to be judged on our sins. We can raise our hands and praise God for his mercy because our sins were taken care of at the cross. But even as believers, we will certainly stand before the Lord to give an account of what we have done with the gifts he has given us. God will not just look at what we have done with our hands; he will also look at our hearts and our motives. These years we spend on earth will really dictate how we spend our eternity with God.

I have some investments in the stock market, in mutual funds, set aside for my retirement. Fortunately, I have about twenty years before I really have to worry about it, but I do think carefully about the investments I am making. How much more should I really be thinking about the investment I am making in eternity, which will go on forever?

As someone has said, "We are placed here to be formed into children of God for all eternity." Are we becoming what he wants us to become? Is Christ truly being formed in us? The Lord will look at our lives, and the answers to those questions will be revealed publicly. What an awesome thought.

## Mercy Is Required of Followers of Jesus

In verse 13 James says, "Judgment without mercy will be shown to anyone who has not been merciful." Into the Roman world of violence and hate, Jesus came preaching that his true followers were going to be people of mercy. It was a requirement then, and it is still a requirement today.

Mercy has never really been too popular. The Romans hated mercy. They considered it a sign of weakness, and they called it "a disease of the soul." They didn't want anyone to be treated with loving-kindness. In fact, if a child was born, and the father didn't want it because it was a girl or because it was deformed, he could have the child killed instantly. Or if a man had a slave he didn't like, he could just give the word, and the slave would be put to death, with no legal repercussions for the owner.

If we think about it, hate and vengeance have always been the preferred choice. Our attitude is not one of grace, mercy, and love, but one that says, "I'll show them; I'll get them back for that." But Jesus requires mercy. Mercy is an aspect of God's love. The New Testament uses three different words for mercy, and the one in this passage conveys the idea of providing relief for someone's misery.

John Chrysostom, one of the early church fathers, said, "Mercy imitates God, and disappoints Satan."[2] God began this idea of mercy, and Jesus carried it out in his ministry. As his followers, we should be like-minded. A Christian *is* something before a Christian *does* something. Mercy is about the action that comes forth when there is love in a person's soul.

Someone has written, "Mercy is unmerited favor from God himself to an erring people who can do nothing to earn it except to hold out their hands."

Raising our hands in prayer shows God that we have nothing in them. It is a sign to him that we are saying: "Father, I cry out to you. I need your mercy. Lord, if it wasn't for your mercy, I could not stand before you." As followers of Jesus, we are to show others the same mercy that we receive from God.

It's said that during the Revolutionary War, George Washington had a close friend, a pastor named Peter Miller. Reverend Miller was having a hard time at his church because of one particular gentleman named Michael Whitman, who agitated the reverend during services and caused him a lot of pain. At one point during the war, Whitman was caught in some treacherous activity and was going to be brought before General Washington to give an account of what he had done. If he were found guilty of treason, he would be put to death.

When Reverend Miller heard of this situation, he decided to walk the seventy miles to talk to his friend, General Washington. When he asked him to pardon Whitman, Washington replied, "No, Peter. I cannot grant you the life of your friend."

Reverend Miller answered, "He's not my friend. He is the bitterest enemy I have."

Washington was stunned. "What? You have walked seventy miles to save the life of an enemy? That puts the matter in a different light. I will grant the pardon."

After this incident, Reverend Miller and Michael Whitman became good friends. The reverend understood mercy. He understood what Jesus wanted him to be.[3]

## Mercy Has Released Us to Accept and Forgive Others

God has been incredibly merciful toward us. He has forgiven us, wiped away our sins, and made us white as snow. If we say that we are followers of Jesus, then we should be treating people in the same way, showing mercy to them even when they don't deserve it. One of the greatest ways that we can show mercy is through forgiveness.

In Matthew 18:21–35, Jesus tells the story of a king who decided to collect from all his debtors. One servant owed him ten thousand talents (several million dollars in today's money), but he could not pay it. So the king forgave the debt. He didn't even say, "You can pay it back later"; he just let him go. Then that servant went and found a fellow servant who owed him a hundred denarii (a few of our dollars). When that man could not pay, the first servant had him thrown into prison until he could pay the debt.

When the king heard what had happened, he was very angry, and he immediately had his servant thrown into jail to be tortured until he could pay back what he owed. Jesus used this story to say that if we don't show mercy to others, God will not be merciful to us.

We seem to enjoy harboring a little anger and bitterness toward people. We like to soak it up and think about how we were right and they were wrong. Revenge seems so sweet, and we have a thousand reasons why we are justified in thinking that way. But James is clear that if we do not show mercy, mercy will not be shown to us.

Jesus did not suggest that we forgive one another. He didn't insinuate it, or give us an encouraging smile and say, "You really should forgive each other." He commanded it. We are like the servant who owed millions of dollars. We owed God a debt we could never repay, and yet he forgave us of it. Now we are obliged to do the same for those who are in debt to us. It is a mark of a true follower of Jesus to let the anger and bitterness go and to say, "I forgive."

In 1996, a Vietnamese woman named Kim was invited to speak at the Vietnam War Memorial in Washington, D.C., for a Veterans Day ceremony. She had been burned by napalm bombs during the Vietnam War when she was a little girl. Amazingly, she survived, thanks to fourteen months in the hospital and seventeen operations. She became very depressed later in her life because of her injuries, until someone invited her to church and she found Jesus. In her speech she said, "It was the fire bomb that burned my body. It was the skill of the doctor that mended my skin, but it took the power of God to heal my heart."

As Kim looked out over the sea of American uniforms, she said, "I have suffered a lot, both physical and emotional pain. Sometimes I thought I could not live, but God saved my life, and he gave me faith and hope. Even if I could talk face to face with the pilot who dropped the bomb, I could tell him, 'We cannot change history, but we should try to do good things for the present and for the future to promote peace.'"[4] Kim had the amazing ability to forgive and move forward.

The royal law of love is, "Do to others as you would have them do to you" (Luke 6:31). That law of love brings forth mercy, which brings forth forgiveness. Because of God's mercy, we have experienced forgiveness, and our sins are not held against us. True faith—real faith—causes us to forgive others.

## CHAPTER 12

# YOU GOTTA HAVE FAITH

### JAMES 2:14–19

A tourist is walking along the edge of the Grand Canyon. He gets a little too close and slips off the edge, but manages to grab a little shrub on his way down. As he hangs there above the canyon, he looks up to heaven and calls, "Is there anybody up there who can help me?"

A calm, powerful voice answers, "Yes, there is someone up here, and I can help you. Do you have faith?"

"Yes, I have very strong faith," the man replies.

"Then let go of the bush."

After a tense pause, the tourist looks back up to the sky and says, "Is there anyone else up there who can help me?"

Having faith is not always easy. Especially when we are dealing with the kind of faith James is talking about in this passage.

## Faith Is Relying on God

In the early church there were false teachers who said that faith was all that was needed for salvation. A believer's lifestyle didn't matter; the way he treated his fellow Christians didn't matter. All that mattered was that he had faith.

James says that works done out of love are evidence of faith, for faith is active.

What kind of faith is James talking about? The word *faith* is used in a variety of ways in Scripture, but it normally means "belief" and "trust." It is a reliance on God and a commitment to his Word.

Faith is a key doctrine of the Christian life, because we are saved by faith, and we walk by faith. It is important that we have the right kind of faith. In this passage, we will see three things faith leads to: works, surrender, and growth and service.

## Real Faith Leads to Works

The sixteenth-century theologian Martin Luther had a problem with the book of James. He was especially concerned about this passage on faith and works. Luther spoke out against the Roman Catholic Church because of its corrupt theology. While studying Romans 1:17, he saw that a person is justified by faith and faith alone. The indulgences, which the Catholic Church sold, had no power to forgive sins. When he voiced his opinions, however, he found himself in hot water.

Luther was chair of biblical studies at Wittenberg University when he first began to grapple with this new concept of faith. He later wrote: "Then I grasped that the justice of God is that righteousness by which, through grace and sheer mercy, God justifies us through faith. Thereupon I felt myself to be reborn and to have gone through open doors into paradise."[1]

Luther realized that the church could not save him, nor would his good deeds be enough to earn salvation. He was going to be saved, made right with God, solely by faith in what Jesus Christ had done for him on that cross.

Luther looked at this passage in James (as you may have) and thought, "Do Paul and James disagree with each other? Paul teaches that salvation is by faith alone. James says that faith is dead without works. Is this a contradiction?"

The answer is absolutely not. In reality, Paul and James complement each other.

First of all, Paul is speaking of pre-conversion, and James is speaking of post-conversion. Paul is pointing out that a person's works are not going to get him into heaven; salvation comes only through a personal relationship with Jesus Christ. On the other hand, James is saying that if a person truly has that relationship, if his faith is real, if he is indeed a follower of Jesus, then his life will naturally show his faith. As that individual walks with Christ, his life will display the fruit of the Spirit through his works.

In Ephesians 2:8–9 Paul says, "For it is by grace you have been saved, through faith—and this not from yourselves, it is the gift of God—not of works, so that no one can boast." That phrase, "this not from yourselves," has created plenty of controversy over the years. Some would argue that this proves that works are not necessary for salvation. However, if we read on, we will see that in verse 10 Paul says, "For we are God's workmanship, created in Christ Jesus to do good works, which God prepared in advance for us to do."

Paul knew the importance of works. However, he wanted to point out that a person's works cannot gain him eternal life. That comes only through faith in Jesus Christ.

However, once a person has made that decision, his life will show it by his works, the things he does for others. That is why James is saying, "What good is it, my brothers, if a man claims to have faith but has no deeds?" (2:14).

## Real Faith Leads to Surrender

I had the opportunity to hear Os Guinness, one of the great thinkers of our time, speak in Amsterdam several years ago. He presented four levels that must be consciously or unconsciously built in us in order for us to have healthy faith.

First, we must be aware of our dilemma without God. This is the point in life where we say, "I'm at the end of my rope. I can't save myself. God, I need you."

Second, we must be aware that if Christianity is true, it is the answer to this dilemma.

Third, we must be aware that Christianity is indeed true. That is the step of faith.

Fourth, we must be prepared to choose Christianity and commit ourselves to the consequences of the choice. This means believing not just with our emotions, but also with our wills. Intellect alone does not save us.

James mentions that even the demons believe in God. Obviously they are not followers of Jesus. They believe in their minds, but they have not activated their wills to follow Jesus in any way. They have not surrendered.

When I think of surrender, I recall the words to the hymn "I Surrender All":

> All to Jesus I surrender, All to Him I freely give;
> I will ever love and trust Him, In His presence daily live....

> All to Jesus I surrender, Humbly at His feet I bow;
> Worldly pleasures all forsaken, Take me, Jesus, take me now....

> All to Jesus I surrender, Lord, I give myself to Thee;
> Fill me with Thy love and power, Let Thy blessings fall on me.[2]

As Americans, we often have trouble with the concept of surrendering. The idea of handing over our wills to God blatantly contradicts the ideas of our society. The mantra, "Nobody is going to tell me what to do!" is as American as baseball, hot dogs, and Mom's apple pie.

We don't want to give up our wills. It's not our intent to surrender. We don't want someone telling us what to do. Very few of us can honestly say, "I surrender all."

Today, when we hear that a family is going to Africa to be missionaries, we often look at them with pity and say, "Oh, that's too bad. You'll have to give up so much that you have here in the States." A hundred years ago, they would have been honored, revered, and respected. Somewhere our thinking has been messed up.

I have a friend in San Diego whose daughter works for the CIA. I can tell he is very proud of her. Of course it's a big deal—how many people do we know who work for the CIA? But how much more should we be proud of our friends and family who go to the mission field or devote their lives to ministry? They aren't just working for top government officials; they are working for God, the Ruler of the universe, the Creator of all things.

If God called us to a faraway place to serve him, would we go? Could we surrender our wills? To surrender means to honestly say, "God, here I am. I'm going to stop living for myself. It's not about my will. It's about you and what you want me to do." We may have known God for a long time; we may be really moved by the praise songs or hymns we sing, and have good feelings for God, but now it's time to activate our wills and truly follow him.

Andrew Murray, a South African missionary, wrote, "We find the Christian life so difficult because we seek for God's blessing while we live in our own will. We would be glad to live the Christian life according to our own liking."[3]

This is a huge issue because there are churches in America that are filled with people on Sunday who have no intention of doing anything for God during the week. They sit back and listen to the sermon, but they rarely take it and apply it to their lives.

If you and I prayed the sinner's prayer when we were six years old, and nothing has happened since then, if we have had no growth or change, then we had better stop and examine our hearts. Did our faith ever move beyond the knowledge of God into the will to actively serve him?

In Matthew 7, Jesus warns against people who claim his name but who do not bear good fruit. He reminds us, "Not everyone who says to me, 'Lord, Lord,' will enter the kingdom of heaven, but only he who does the will of my Father who is in heaven" (2:21).

Just because we prayed a prayer when we were a child (or an adult), does not necessarily mean we have a free ticket to heaven. That is not real faith. Saving faith activates the intellect, the emotions, and the will. That kind of faith says, "Yes, I will follow Jesus."

## Real Faith Leads to Growth and Service

Several years ago, I went to the doctor for some heart problems. The medical technicians strapped an "event monitor" to my chest that I had to wear for two weeks. Whenever something didn't feel quite right in my heart, I would push a button, and the machine would record what was going on in my chest. Different things would aggravate the problem—turbulence on an airplane, or the times when I got angry. Trips to Starbucks sent it off the charts.

After two weeks, the technicians hooked up the monitor to a machine to see what the results were. It was a little scary to realize that someone was going to see what had been going on inside of me.

Do you realize that God monitors hearts? You and I have a spiritual "event monitor" on us, and we don't even know it. We can try to slide through this Christian life as though everything is wonderful, yet God is looking at our hearts. He knows what our intentions are.

James tells us that faith without works, faith without change, faith without mercy, is not real faith at all. It's bogus faith. And only we and God know whether our faith is real or not.

That is why the Bible talks about spiritual gifts. Every Christian should be serving; every believer should be giving. Jesus should be affecting every area of our lives, our time, and our money.

With God's rich mercy and his incredible love, why wouldn't we want to surrender to him? We know he loves us. We know he is looking out for our best interests. So why do we wrestle with this issue? Why don't we just surrender it all because he knows what's best for us? Who is going to take care of us better than God?

My prayer for you is that you are able to experience the excitement of seeing spiritual growth in your life. Nothing is more satisfying than denying self and saying yes to God.

## CHAPTER 13

# HOW BIG ARE YOUR THOUGHTS?

*JAMES 2:20–24*

In Mark 9:17–27, a father who loved his son very much was in agony. For some reason his son could not speak. His child was plagued by epileptic seizures, which caused him to convulse on the floor and foam at the mouth. He had taken his son to Jesus' disciples, and they could not help him. It seemed that there was no hope for the boy.

But then this distraught father brought his son to see Jesus. Jesus asked how long the boy had been that way; the father told him the evil spirit causing the seizures had been with the boy since childhood. He said that the spirit often threw the boy into the fire or into water. "Take pity on us and help us," the father pleaded (2:22).

Jesus told the man that everything is possible for him who believes. Immediately, the father answered, "I do believe; help me overcome my unbelief!" (2:24).

Have you ever called out, "God, help me in my unbelief"? When the father asked Jesus, "Can you help us?" he used the word *help* that means "instantaneous help." He wanted his son cured right away. But the second time he used the word *help*, it was the word that means "a continuous help." He was saying, "Lord, I believe, but I need you to help me keep growing, because my faith is so small."

Not only do we need faith at the point of salvation, we also need it in our daily living. Every morning that we wake up we need faith, so that we can abide with Jesus in every situation we encounter.

## Faith Is Made Complete by Works

Someone once said, "We can't choose our relatives, but we can choose our thoughts, and those influence us much more."

James is pointing out in this passage that faith must be accompanied by action. Talk is cheap. Anybody can say, "Yes, I'm a Christian," without having any evidence to back it up. No growth, no change, no renewal.

James uses this illustration. Suppose a person comes to us, naked and hungry, and we give the typical Jewish response, "Go in peace!" What have we really done for that needy individual?

When we see someone with a need, what do we say to him or her? "I'll be praying for you," is a typical response. James says that's not enough. If we are truly followers of Jesus, when we see a brother or sister in need, we have to do something about that need.

James brings up Abraham. If you know the story, you will remember that God came to Abraham and asked him to present his son Isaac as a sacrifice. Abraham proceeded to do as God asked, and in the end God saved his son (see Genesis 22:1–18). James says about Abraham, "His faith and his actions were working together, and his faith was made complete by what he did" (2:22).

James concludes that "a person is justified by what he does and not by faith alone" (2:24). Wait a minute! Is he directly contradicting what Paul teaches? Actually James is using the word *justified* in a different way. Besides meaning to be proven right or just, the word can also mean "that aspect of judgment," as in Matthew 12:37 where Jesus says, "For by your words you will be justified, and by your words you will be condemned" (NASB).

Abraham's faith was judged by his actions. When God asked him to do what seemed unthinkable, he did it. Abraham proved his faith by his works. How could Abraham be willing to give up his only son? One reason is that he had great thoughts about God.

## Faith Begins and Ends with Thoughts about God

As we read through the book of Psalms, we see God's greatness, his power, his love, his presence, his majesty, and his compassion; it causes our thoughts about God to continue to grow. How do we have faith? By having big thoughts about God. By understanding what he is capable of doing.

Our thoughts are really what drives our faith. Someone has said, "You are not what you think you are. What you think, you are." That is so true when it comes to how we view God.

Gandhi had a favorite saying regarding the Christians of Great Britain. He said, "If Christians would really live according to the teachings of Christ, as found in the Bible, all of India would be Christian today."[1] The way we live reveals what we believe about God. It shows whether we have big thoughts or small thoughts about God.

Thoughts run through our heads all day long. We create ideas, images, and scenarios about how our lives will go. In our minds, we have also created an image of God. Our faith begins and ends with our thoughts about him.

A person can live without air for a few minutes, without water for a few days, and without food for a few weeks. Sadly, though, we can live year after year without having a new thought about God and about his greatness and majesty.

How could Abraham raise up that knife to kill his son? He had great thoughts about God. I wonder—how great are our thoughts about God?

## Faith Doesn't Keep God in a Box

When I came to the Lord, I wanted to grow in my faith. As I read the Bible, I discovered that God could do incredible things. But instead of being encouraged, I was disappointed to hear my professors say, "No, God doesn't do that anymore. He doesn't speak like that or heal like that." They put God in a box; they seemed to love their systematic theology more than they loved God himself.

We define and explain God by our thoughts and words. We tell people, "This is what God does and doesn't do." Why have we reduced the Christian life to whatever we can explain? Why have we rejected the supernatural? God is too big to be confined by our limited ability to explain him.

I was sitting in a hotel room in Orissa, a state of India, during a crisis point in my life. I was reading in the gospel of Mark about power, healing, and intimacy with God. As I looked out my window, I could see dozens of people with a variety of problems—some were blind, some were lame, some were deaf. I began to think, "Why can't this same power I'm reading about in Mark be unleashed right here in India?"

At that moment I came very close to giving up. As I sat there in that hotel room looking at my Bible and looking at my life, I realized that the two did not match up. I wanted to walk away from it all.

In 1995, things began to change. I began to talk to God honestly. I said, "Father, let's start from scratch. Lord, I want to know you and the power of your resurrection. I want to know Jesus, and I want to be filled with your Spirit. I don't want to just talk about you; I want to know you. I want to cling to you, not to a doctrine, a creed, or a system. I want to know you deeply." I determined then that no one would ever tell me again what to think about God.

God blows away the boxes we may try to put him in. He is bigger than our finite minds; he goes far beyond what we can think or imagine (see Ephesians 3:20). Through his prophet he says to us, "My thoughts are not your thoughts, neither are your ways my ways" (Isaiah 55:8).

Abraham had great thoughts about God. He had a great vision of who God is. His faith kept growing. So here James is telling his readers, "You may say you have faith, but if you're not stepping out and doing things to help others, your faith is dead!"

## Faith Requires Stepping Out

Several years ago while my dad and I were talking on the telephone he asked me, "If you could do anything with your life, what would you do?"

I thought about it and said, "I would start my own ministry organization."

"So what's keeping you?" he asked.

After I hung up the phone, I thought for a while about his question. Why couldn't I start one? The answer was one little word: *fear*. My view of God was so dinky, so pathetic, so ungodly. I thought he would let me get out there, walking on the water, and then let me sink and drown. Finally, I went to God in prayer and said, "Father, I'm so sorry. I have made you so small. I have given you so little room to work in me. Forgive me. Give me new thoughts."

There have been times when I have lost my faith—not my salvation faith, but my daily faith—because my thoughts about God were so small. The good news is that we don't have to stay with those small thoughts.

Ask God to give you great thoughts about him. Don't let a preconceived idea tell you what God can and cannot do. Let him show you his greatness and his power.

Faith isn't easy. I am learning that fact. As an analytical person, I like to say, "I'll do this; I'll change that. It'll work." But things don't always happen the way we plan. We don't always know how God will direct our paths.

I did start my own ministry organization. I looked my fear in the eye and said, "Okay, God, you're bigger than this." I put God to the test, and he humbled me and took me where I never thought I could go. Rather than let me founder, God picked me up and said, "You stepped out in faith; now I'll take you the rest of the way."

You may have been at a crisis point before in your life. You may be there right now. If so, I encourage you to read what the psalmists say about God, about the bigness and majesty of our Creator. Review the things he has done in the past, and then trust him for the future.

In the Jewish culture, people are always retelling stories of the great things that God has done. They often sit down with their families and begin, "You remember how God parted the Red Sea?" Or they smile as they ask, "Do you know how God saved our people from the Philistines?"

We need our own stories like that. What a testimony to be able to sit down with our families and say, "Do you remember when God did this for us?"

I don't know about you, but I don't want to live on someone else's faith experience. True, I can read about Hudson Taylor and some of the other giants of the Christian faith, and be encouraged by their lives. But God has done so much in my own life! I want my faith in him to be built up because I stepped out in faith, and he proved to be faithful.

I pray that you feel the same way and that you too will step out in faith, trusting totally in God to prove himself faithful in your life.

## CHAPTER 14

# LORD, HELP ME BELIEVE

## JAMES 2:23–26

A college student wants to work his way through school so he decides to go door to door looking for odd jobs. He goes to a very affluent neighborhood, walks up to a nice house, and knocks on the door. When a man answers it, the student says, "Good morning, sir. I'm trying to work my way through college by doing odd jobs. Do you have anything I could do?"

"That's great. I love to see a college student with enthusiasm to work," the man answers. "I'll give you fifty dollars to paint my porch. There's a can of green paint back by the shed."

The student works hard painting, and when he is finally done, he comes back to the door and knocks. When the man sees him there, sweating and covered in green paint, he says, "Wow, you really worked hard. I'm going to give you a bonus. Here's a hundred dollars for painting my porch."

"Great, thanks," says the college student. "I really appreciate it." Then as he starts to walk away, he turns back and says, "Oh, by the way, that's not a Porsche out back. It's a Ferrari."

This man had faith that the college student knew what he was doing. Unfortunately, his faith was ill placed.

To God it is not enough for us to simply say, "Yes, I have Jesus in my heart," and then do nothing to prove it. Our faith is important in activating our wills, in motivating and inspiring us to do something for God.

Faith begins and ends with our thoughts about God. How big

we think God is determines what we do for him by faith. We have looked at the example of Abraham, who, because he stepped out in faith, "was called God's friend" (2:23). James says that a person is justified by what he does, and not by his faith alone. In other words, talk is cheap.

## Faith Is Not Void of Emotion

Abraham was not a robot. In Genesis 22:1–2, when God told Abraham to take his son Isaac and offer him on the altar, Abraham certainly had some heavy emotions weighing on his heart. He couldn't just say to God, "Okay, whatever you say, Lord," and not feel any doubt, any insecurity, or any pain. He loved his son, and he was probably thinking, *What in the world is God asking me to do?*

Emotions are generated by thoughts. Abraham had emotions, but he also had great thoughts about God. He allowed his thoughts to dwell on God's awesomeness and power, and he was able to step out in faith and say, "Okay, God, I'm going to do whatever you say, because I know that you are great and powerful and that you will get me through this situation."

Some people let their emotions control every aspect of their lives. Every decision, every response, everything they do is an emotional roller coaster. They have emotional highs, where everything is great; then they have emotional lows, where everything is very dark. It can be a very unhealthy way to live.

People have asked me, "Dan, are you always high?" I actually have times when I get very low, and I struggle through dark periods. But every time that happens, I can trace it back to my thinking. I have had shallow or weak thoughts about God. I have put God back in a box again. I have said, "God, you can't do that. You don't love me enough to do that for me. I know you won't take care of me." I realize that every time I allow negative images into my mind, negative emotions soon follow.

You may be without a job right now. Perhaps you are thinking, *There's no hope. I'm never going to get a job. Nobody is ever going to want to hire me.* When you start thinking that way, your emotions begin to follow that thinking, and pretty soon you are spiraling down a pathway of negativity. Some of us do that on a fairly regular basis. We continue to spiral down, and we suffer from depression because of our thinking and the images we have created in our minds.

I once read an editorial that said:

> The world is too big for us. Too much going on, too many crimes, too much violence and excitement. Try as you will, you get behind in the race, in spite of yourself. It's an incessant strain to keep pace and still you lose ground. Science empties its discoveries on you so fast that you stagger beneath them in hopeless bewilderment. The political world is news seen so rapidly that you're out of breath trying to keep pace with who's in and who's out. Everything is high pressure. Human nature can't endure much more.

Interestingly enough, that editorial was published in the *Atlantic Journal* in the 1830s.[1] The world hasn't changed much for people who look at life with dark emotions.

If we look at everything in a negative way, if we take God out of every situation, we will never do anything for him. Living faith is that faith that causes us to step out, that faith that causes us to activate our wills in obedience to God.

## Our Faith Grows as We Grow

Taylor, my five-year-old, informed me one day that he does not want to grow. He said he is going to stay small forever because he doesn't want to go to school. (I think his brothers have been "discipling" him.) But the truth is, we all grow up, and so does our faith.

As we look at Abraham's life, we can see that his faith was not always what we read in these verses from James. Twice he lied about his wife being his sister (see Genesis 12:10–13; 20:1–2). He had failures, and there were situations in his life in which he messed up, but he always learned something new about God. God tested him, and his knowledge of God increased. His faith grew, not because he read a bunch of books about God, but because he experienced God personally. Faith does not end with salvation. It continues to grow throughout our entire lives.

I recently took my wife Deb to see the doctor, and he had to do a battery of tests. The doctor explained that he was going to do a procedure in which he would shove a tube down her throat, look at her esophagus, and cut something out of it. He painted a pretty gruesome picture, and how did she respond? She didn't ask, "Can I see your credentials? Can you give me some references? Have you ever done this before?" She just said, "Okay, whatever you need to do."

Her faith has grown. She has delivered three children and had her gallbladder removed; each time the doctor told her what would happen, and it was successful. So she wasn't concerned when the doctor explained what he was going to do. She trusted that it would work out.

Our faith needs to grow. As long as we try to control God, our faith is stagnant. It is when he takes us into the deep waters that our faith grows. Sometimes we just have to say, "I don't know how this is going to work out; I don't have all the answers to this situation; but I am going to trust God." That's when our faith grows.

So when God asked Abraham to sacrifice his only son, Abraham said, "Okay, Lord, whatever you want," and raised the knife. Then God said, "Hold it right there. I just wanted to see if you are growing. I wanted to know if you really trust me, if you really have your faith grounded in me" (see Genesis 22:9–12).

In his encounter with the Roman centurion, Jesus said, "I have not found anyone in Israel with such great faith" (Matthew 8:10). When he calmed the storm for his disciples, he said, "Where is your faith?" (Luke 8:25). To the blind men who asked him to heal them, he said, "According to your faith will it be done to you" (Matthew 9:29). Faith is important to God.

To see God as he is, to be able to put our trust in him, we must learn to say, "I don't know where this is going to lead me, but I'm going to step out anyway." That is why we need to think big thoughts about God.

I love the story in Mark 2:1–12 about the four men who low-ered their paralytic friend down through a roof into a house where Jesus was teaching. When Jesus saw their faith, he healed the man. Those four guys had a lot of faith to go through all the trouble of lowering a man through a roof. That is the kind of "roof-raising" faith that God is looking for today.

God is looking for people who will say, "I don't have all the answers, but I'm going to step out in faith. I'm going to dream something for you, Lord, and I believe with all of my heart you can give me this dream." We stop dreaming because we don't believe God can really do what we envision. We think that the God of the Bible is gone, that he doesn't do miracles anymore.

If you have never seen the movie *Rudy*, you need to see it. It is the story of a young man who wanted to play football at Notre Dame from the time he was little. However, he was dyslexic, and everyone told him that he wouldn't be able to do it. Instead of lis-tening to them, he took off for Notre Dame, even though he hadn't been accepted. While he was there, he ran into a priest who was actually a former president of the school. As he shared his story, Rudy said, "This is what I want to do. Everyone has said I can't do it, but I'm going to go for it."

Rudy actually enrolled in Notre Dame and went out for the football team. All he could do was play on the practice squad because he was so small compared to the other guys. But on the last game of his last year, he got to go out on the field and see his dream become a reality.

What is your dream? Do you have one? Did you have one but lost it? Faith is important, not just saving faith, but living faith.

## Our Words Reveal Our Faith

Let's take a look at the example of Rahab in James 2, verse 25. Rahab was the opposite of Abraham. Here we have the patriarch and the prostitute, a hero and a hooker. But God worked in the lives of both of them.

Joshua sent spies into the city of Jericho, and Rahab hid them and helped them escape from the men who were trying to find them—her own neighbors. She made a deal with the spies. "I'll help you escape, but when you come back and wipe out this city, please remember me." They agreed.

In Joshua 2:9, 11, we see exactly what Rahab was thinking:

> I know that the LORD has given this land to you and that a great fear of you has fallen on us, so that all who live in this country are melting in fear because of you.... When we heard of it, our hearts melted and everyone's courage failed because of you, for the LORD your God is God in heaven above and on the earth below.

She came to the point where she believed in God, and she showed it by her words.

If we can't point to a time or a situation in which we saw God do something for us, our faith is not growing. We need to get into situations in which the only way out is by God's help. Every time he gets us out, it builds our faith. Hebrews 11:6 says, "Without faith it is impossible to please God." Are we pleasing God by acting on the faith we say we have in him?

James says to his audience, "Faith without works is dead" (2:26). God still says the same thing to us today. We have to go beyond what we think is safe and do what we can only dream of doing. We need to let God out of the box so he can do his job. We need to worship him as God, worship him with our emotions and also with our minds and our wills—faith plus works.

The question is, is it real? I pray that your faith is real to you, not a Sunday morning activity but something that you experience throughout the week. I pray that God will show you his supernatural power, his supernatural work, and his incredible presence as you step out in faith for him.

# DON'T DO AS I DO ... SURE!

### JAMES 3:1–2

A doctor and a lawyer are standing together at a party. As they are talking, a woman comes over and begins asking the doctor some questions about a pain in her leg. Being a nice man, the doctor gives her some advice. After she leaves, the doctor turns to the lawyer and asks, "I just gave her fifteen minutes of my time. Can I bill her for the professional services I just rendered?"

"Certainly," the lawyer replies. "She asked you the same questions a patient would ask her doctor, and you gave her advice."

The next morning the doctor writes out a bill for the woman. At the same time, the lawyer writes a bill for the doctor, charging him for the legal counsel he gave him. The lawyer teaches the doctor something that day: Treat others as you yourself would like to be treated.

In this passage, James is talking to teachers. In a way, we are all teachers. Whether we are in the classroom, at work, at home, or just dealing with people on a daily basis, we are all teaching.

## We Are All Teachers

James begins this new passage on the power of the tongue by addressing one of the problems facing the early church. He gets right to the point and says, "Not many of you should presume to be teachers, my brothers, because you know that we who teach will be judged more strictly" (3:1). The Jewish culture revered places of authority. The office of rabbi held great honor. Many of the Jewish disciples wanted to occupy high positions. James is saying to them, "You had better be careful. A lot of you want to become teachers. Remember that once you become a teacher, you are going to be held accountable for the things that come out of your mouth."

James had been with Jesus, and he knew the importance of living a life that matches one's words. James was not interested in just acquiring or dispensing knowledge. He was interested in the same thing that Jesus was interested in—transforming lives. The Jewish leaders were interested in transformation to some degree, but they also loved giving out facts and sharing information.

While I was in Poland to speak at a conference, I stayed with a Jewish family who spoke English and loved to talk. They shared with me various bits of information from Jewish history, and we discussed different issues in the Bible. One morning I asked them, "Do all Jews believe in God?" The father began, "No, not all Jews believe in God. There are Jews who are atheists, and there are Jews who are Communists." Then he continued speaking for thirty or forty minutes.

In the early church, everyone wanted to become a teacher. Many of them were not ready. They were not qualified. They did not have the life experience. Some of them did not have the gift. Many scholars feel that James is referring here to people who are anxious to share what they know in everyday settings, like the Jewish family I stayed with in Poland.

## Teach as Jesus Taught

I recently read a book called *Jesus, the Pastor* by John Frye. The book explains that we train our pastors to teach by looking at the Pauline epistles, without ever looking to see how Jesus taught. We say that we want to follow him and emulate him. If that is so, then we need to ask ourselves: "How did Jesus teach? What was important to Jesus as he ministered on earth?"

Frye says, "Jesus Christ defined teaching as training for a way of life, not as transferring information from one mind to another."[1] After most ministerial students get out of seminary, the original fire to see people come to the Lord has usually diminished somewhat.

Over a period of time, that simple passion goes by the wayside, and is replaced by the dissection of Scripture and the search for deeper and deeper meaning.

Jesus said, "A student is not above his teacher, but everyone who is fully trained will be like his teacher" (Luke 6:40). Teaching is not about having all the answers (or thinking we do). It's about a new life with God. Its purpose is not to impart knowledge, but to bring people into a closer walk with God, a new experience with the living Lord.

Most of us don't need more knowledge. Instead, the knowledge that we have needs to be acted upon. We are not going to become better Christians by getting more knowledge. What's the point of studying the Bible if we can't take Jesus' most basic commands and live them out? We are going to become better Christians, better followers of Jesus, by simply saying, "Okay, Lord, I'm going to submit to you. I'm going to do what you tell me to do."

In his book, Frye gives a great analogy: If we go on a road trip, we will probably have a map with us. It will tell us where to go and where we can stop to get something to eat or use the restroom. But the thrill is not getting to know the map. The thrill is the journey, the experience, and finally getting to our destination.

Should we study God's Word, the map? Absolutely, because we would be lost without it. It tells us where we are going and how to get there. However, our final destination is God. Our goal should not be to memorize the map, but to come to know and experience the one to whom it leads (see John 5:39–40).

In verse 2, James says, "We all stumble in many ways." He is being very transparent here. The early Christians were having a problem because they liked the places of authority. Because they desired so desperately to be in high positions, they often created divisions. James is reminding them, and us, that we are all teachers, and we are all going to stumble.

## Even Teachers Must Continue to Learn

A pottery teacher divided his class into two groups. He told one group that they would be graded on how many pieces of pottery they completed. If they made fifty pieces of pottery, they would get an A; if they made forty pieces, they would get a B; and so on. Then he told the other half of the class that their grades would be based on quality instead of quantity. On the last day, they would present one piece that would determine their entire grade.

At the end of the semester, those students who had churned out many pots had learned something new each week from their failures and their successes. Those who were going to be graded on just one piece became stuck because they were so worried about getting it perfect. The first group learned by trial and error, and their work was much better than that of the second group. They learned by growing and experiencing.

Unfortunately, in our Christian lives we sometimes think, "I've got all the answers now. I've read the Bible through a dozen times, and there's nothing left to learn." No matter how old or how knowledgeable we get, we can always continue to learn and grow.

Many times, I have heard pastors say, "Well, I've come to see things in a different light," or, "I have a different perspective on that passage now," or, "My theology has changed over the years." In other words, they have grown. They have grown in knowledge, experience, and understanding, just like the church fathers we so often quote. Their ideas have changed as they have gained new insights.

The saddest thing is people who have stopped learning. Even the apostle Paul, at the end of his life, asked Timothy to bring his parchments to him; he still had more to learn about God (2 Timothy 4:13). Regardless of our age or our knowledge, if we have the Spirit of God dwelling in us we can still learn, still grow and develop mentally and spiritually.

There was a time in my life when I saw everything as black and white. That was the way I had been taught, and it was easy. Anybody who disagreed with my theology was wrong. Through the years, the Holy Spirit has begun to show me that there are some areas of gray. I don't like gray. Gray is hard. Gray means I have to wrestle with things. Gray means I have to go to bed a little uneasy at night.

As a pastor, I often have to deal with situations that aren't black and white. There is a right and a wrong, but there is usually some gray mixed in both sides. Even though that situation can be unsettling at times, it always draws me closer to the Lord and helps me realize that I don't have all the answers.

We all teach and, as teachers, we must all continue to grow. Nobody can force us to grow. The Holy Spirit accomplishes that work in our lives.

I had many teachers in seminary who taught their students exactly what they had been taught. They had a syllabus, and they stuck to it. When asked a question by one of their students, they would simply quote from the syllabus. But every once in a while, I would have a brave teacher who was still learning, still asking questions, and who, when asked a question, would honestly say, "I don't know the answer to that one."

In all my years of education, I can count on one hand the teachers I have had who taught like Jesus. But there was one I will never forget. It was in high school, the first Christian school I ever attended. I walked into Mr. Keller's class and saw a man who radiated Christ. Every day he would tell us stories of how he had stopped and talked to someone and led him or her to Christ. Any student could raise his hand and tell him about a problem, and he would stop right in the middle of class and pray for that student.

Mr. Keller has always been an example to me of a man who taught like Jesus. He wasn't rude, mean, or "in your face." He didn't simply give us information; he showed us a life of complete commitment to Christ.

There are all kinds of teachers. We all have different gifts. But let's not forget that teaching is not just about imparting information. A good teacher will live a transformed life, one that will make people say, "That person knows Jesus."

Here in this passage James is saying to us, "You want to be a teacher? Then you had better walk the way Jesus walked." In 1 John 2:5–6 the writer says of Jesus, "This is how we know we are in him: Whoever claims to live in him must walk as Jesus did."

Too many of us have stopped trying to learn. We are stuck, just like those pottery students, trying to make the perfect life. God is calling us to step out in faith, to walk with him. Let's have the same passion that Jesus had to transform lives.

# HOW ARE YOU AT GIVING DIRECTIONS?

*JAMES 3:3–5*

A woman and her neighbor get into a conversation about recipes. The first woman mentions a fantastic recipe for meatloaf. "I have to give you this recipe," she gushes. "It's great. Every time I mention to my husband that I'm going to make meatloaf for dinner, he says, 'You have been working hard all day. Let me take you out for dinner.' So anytime you don't want to cook, just mention this recipe to your husband, and he'll take you out for dinner with no complaints!"

The power of words is incredible. They have the power to encourage, and the power to discourage, the power to liberate, and the power to manipulate. Although they can't be physically seen or felt, their power is immense. In this passage, James gives us some illustrations of the power of the tongue.

## The Tongue Does Not Act Alone

Think about your tongue. Wiggle it around a little. That muscle in your mouth isn't moving on its own. You have to tell it to do its job. Your brain sends the messages to your tongue, but the instructions come from your heart. Bits alone do not control horses. The rudder by itself does not control a ship. People use bits or rudders to accomplish what they desire. So it is with the tongue.

Jesus reminds us in Luke 6:45, "The good man brings good things out of the good stored up in his heart, and the evil man brings evil things out of the evil stored up in his heart. For out of

109

the overflow of his heart his mouth speaks." We don't normally say something unless we have already thought it.

Our words reveal what is already in our hearts. That is the scariest thing about words. Whether it's in our homes, at work, with friends, or at church, whenever we speak, we reveal what is stored up inside us. The tongue does not act alone. Our words come from a deeper source—our hearts.

Blaise Pascal wrote, "Cold words freeze people, and hot words scorch them, and bitter words make them bitter, and wrathful words make them wrathful. Kind words also produce their own image on men's souls and a beautiful image it is."[1]

We could talk a lot about the negative impact that our words can have on people. But there is also tremendous power in the positive side of speech. When a person is walking in the Spirit, the way he or she uses words to encourage others is wonderful. However, it's not just the words that are important. It's also the spirit in which the words are spoken. Listeners can tell a lot from tone and inflection.

In all my experiences of traveling around the world, I have never been to a country that has had a crueler or more inhumane dictator than Romania had under Communism. Nicolae Ceausescu was a man of absolute cruelty. The torture and suffering that the Christians in Romania have endured is overwhelming. Even ten years later, I still hear the stories of the horrible things the people of Romania have experienced.

I think of a man named Bardo who was serving a death sentence in a prison in Romania. He was once a prominent prosecuting attorney and a member of the Communist party. Overnight, he went from occupying a position of wealth and importance to starving in a labor camp. The camp's purpose was to keep prisoners on the edge of death at all times.

One afternoon he was sitting in the labor camp, weak and hungry, when a fellow prisoner came to him and offered him some of his food. Bardo couldn't believe that this man would share his food, but he graciously took it. He asked curiously, "How long are you going to be in this prison?"

"I'm here for twenty years," the man answered.

"What crime did you commit?" Bardo asked.

"I was sentenced for giving food to a fugitive pastor. Because of that, they put me in prison."

Bardo noticed that the man did not have the anger or bitterness that most of the other prisoners had. He hesitantly asked, "So who put you in here?"

"Sir, you were the state prosecutor at my trial. You probably don't recognize me, but I remember you. Back then, I wished that someday you might realize that it is right and good to give food to a hungry man, even if it's an enemy. Now I can show you. I am a Christian, and Christ taught us to repay evil with good."

That day, Bardo was on the way to meeting Jesus Christ. It wasn't the words that the prisoner shared with him; it was the spirit in which he shared them.[2]

The words that come out of our mouths generate from what is in our hearts. The tongue doesn't act by itself. Love and forgiveness were in that prisoner's heart. The Spirit of Christ enabled him to give bread to the man who had put him in prison for twenty years.

## The Big Power of the Little Tongue

In this passage, James gives us two fabulous illustrations. First, he uses the analogy of the bit, which controls the body and the will of the horse. I have ridden four horses in my life, and I will never ride another one. I don't like horses. There is really one reason. They can think, and that makes me very nervous. Horses have brains and wills, and every horse that I have ever ridden has acted demon possessed. I would much rather ride a brainless motorcycle, because I know that my will can overcome its engine. Some people have the skill, though, to ride horses with grace and ease. They can use that tiny bit to control the horse and direct it where they want it to go.

The other illustration James uses deals with a boat. Now I like sailing. I can control a boat with that little rudder, no matter how strong the winds are. To put the analogy in today's terms, think of a computer chip. An entire airplane, or a space shuttle, is controlled by one tiny chip containing all the information needed to fly the aircraft.

The tongue is a small muscle, but it boasts great things. Proverbs 18:21 says, "The tongue has the power of life and death, and those who love it will eat its fruit." How do we have the power of life and death in our mouths? Look at Romans 10:9–10: "If you confess with your mouth, 'Jesus is Lord,' and believe in your heart that God raised him from the dead, you will be saved. For it is with your heart that you believe and are justified, and it is with your mouth that you confess and are saved." Our words will either convict us or free us (see Matthew 12:37). We believe in our hearts, and our words confess what we believe.

The second half of Proverbs 18:21 says, "Those who love it will eat its fruit." If we give out words that are painful, words that are critical, and words that are hurtful, that is what will come back our way. We will reap what we sow (see Galatians 6:7); maybe not next week, or even next year, but eventually we will see the results of the things we have said.

On the positive side, though, if we bring forth words of life, if our words bring healing and encouragement to people, those words will come back to us as well. It may not be today, tomorrow, or next week, but we will reap what we sow.

James says that our words have the power to direct someone's life. In some ways, words determine a person's fate. A jury says, "Guilty" or "Not guilty." A referee says, "In bounds" or "Out of bounds." A friend says, "Good choice" or "Bad choice." Incredibly powerful words come from something as small as the tongue.

## We Will Be Remembered for Our Words

It is always interesting to officiate at funerals and hear what people say about the person who died. What we say during our lives is often what we will be remembered for after we die.

One day I received a letter from Dr. Robert Schuller of the Crystal Cathedral. He is a great man with an incredible ministry. He took time out of his busy day to stop and write me a letter, sharing words of encouragement, Scripture, and a prayer. That letter really caused me to think about the power of a word of encouragement.

Words are potent and powerful. They can inspire hope, or they can destroy dreams. They can start a war, or they can heal a heart. And remember, we will be held accountable for the words that we speak (see Matthew 12:36).

In 1947, a man named Jackie Robinson became the first African American to play major league professional baseball. When the Brooklyn Dodgers drafted him, they took a huge step of faith by being the first team in the majors to let a black man play.

Every time Jackie Robinson went out on the field, he had to deal with a lot of jeering from the people in the stands. They would call him names, and talk about his mother. Every day he had to listen to that kind of verbal harassment. One day it was really getting to him, and he struck out with the bases loaded. He made several fielding errors that he wouldn't normally have made, and the crowd was going crazy. Somebody called time out, and Jackie Robinson was about to walk off the field. He was ready to quit.

A fellow Dodger, Pee Wee Reese, walked out onto the field and put his arm around Jackie's shoulder. He said, in effect, "Jackie, let me tell you something. I believe in you. You are the greatest baseball player I have ever seen. You can do this. One of these days you're going to be in the Hall of Fame, so hold your head up high and play ball like only you can do." The game resumed, and Jackie Robinson ended up hitting the winning run.

In 1962, Jackie Robinson was inducted into the National Baseball Hall of Fame. In his speech, he told that story, saying, "Pee Wee saved my life and career that day. I had lost my confidence, and he picked me up with words of encouragement. He gave me hope when all hope was gone."[3]

As far as I know, Pee Wee Reese did not have the Spirit of God, yet he used his tongue to give life back to another man. He used his words to lift somebody up.

We give direction with our words. I look at my life and wonder, *How am I at directing other people? Am I leading them down the path of self-centeredness along with me? Do I direct them to feelings of anger? Do I direct them to negativity and criticism, or do I inspire them, lift them up, and give them hope? Do I bring words of faith to other people, or do I destroy their faith with my tongue?*

One man told me that I would never be an evangelist. Another man told me that I would definitely be an evangelist. I am glad I listened to the right man. If people are continually bringing you down with their negative words, then you need to do something about it. If you have said things that bring others down, whether it is your spouse, your kids, or your friends, if you have caused pain in the lives of others, you need to go back and ask for forgiveness.

James says that the tongue makes great boasts (3:5). Why? Because it has the power to direct people's lives. Let's give direction, but in an encouraging, uplifting, faith-filled way. May we be people who truly speak the way Jesus spoke.

## CHAPTER 17

# STICKS AND STONES: THE REAL STORY
## JAMES 3:5–12

A s a kid, I hated going to school. School was often a painful experience in my elementary and junior-high years. Teasing, taunting, and criticism made my days long and miserable. One saying was supposed to make me feel better, "Sticks and stones will break my bones, but words will never hurt me."

At eight years of age, that line sounded pretty good, but at forty-eight, I realize how untrue it really is. Sticks and stones leave physical wounds that normally heal after a couple of weeks. But wounds from words can last much longer. Sadly, those wounds sometimes never heal.

I read a book by a psychologist who said that the average person has fifty thousand thoughts a day, and that about half those thoughts are negative. If that statistic is true, it makes for a lot of negative conversation.

In many ways, we are a very negative people. From talk radio shows to television commercials to political debates, our speech is frequently negative and criticizing.

In our study of James, chapter 3, we have already looked at how the tongue can be used to direct and encourage. Now in this passage we will look at the negative power of the tongue—the power to destroy.

In verses 5–6, James asks us to consider how a great forest can be set on fire with a single spark. He compares this scene to the way our tongues can be a fire within us, corrupting the whole person. There are four characteristics of fire that are also true about the tongue.

## Fire Starts Small

One fire in the history of America was so big it is referred to as the "Great Fire." Religious people of the day thought that the fire was judgment from God. Those of a political persuasion thought it was Communist activity. The common man thought it was started by a cow.

On October 8, 1871, at 8:30 p.m., a fire started in Chicago. It was indeed traced back to the O'Learys' barn. The fire burned for a day and half and just about destroyed the city. More than 17,000 buildings were destroyed, 100,000 people were left homeless, and 300 lives were lost. That great fire started very small. Whether it was started by a lantern kicked over by the O'Learys' cow or not, it only took one flame to set an entire city on fire.[1]

James says that our tongues act in the same way. It may speak only a small word or sentence, but it can start a fire that goes far beyond what we intended. Fire is energy; the words we speak have energy too.

People have probably said things to you or about you that still stick with you. A kid told me in the fifth grade, "Man, you sure are ugly." Now, almost forty years later, I still remember his face and what he said. It has been with me all of my life.

Just as a great fire starts small, our words also start small. When they enter someone's mind and heart, however, they can grow rapidly.

## Fire Grows Rapidly

All a fire needs is fuel and oxygen and it will spread like wildfire—literally. An unattended campfire can consume an entire forest in hours.

I was fishing with some friends at Brannan Island. We inadvertently started a fire that grew out of control on property that belonged to the state of California. I watched helplessly at how fast that fire grew. We couldn't get it out, and we paid dearly for our mistake.

One of the words that the Bible uses in regard to the tongue is *gossip*. It is part of our human nature to gossip—at home, at work, even at church. But this is not how we are to be as Christians. Jesus said, "The good man brings good things out of the good stored up in him, and the evil man brings evil things out of the evil stored up in him. But I tell you that men will have to give account on the day of judgment for every careless word they have spoken" (Matthew 12:35–36).

A rumor spreads just as quickly as gossip does. I have learned that truth in ministry, and I have seen it in my life. There is no such thing as a secret. As soon as something is shared with someone else, it's public. And every time it is retold, the gossip is mutated until it barely resembles the original comment.

My wife came home one night, laughing as she came through the door. "Do you want to hear the latest gossip from church?" she asked. I shrugged my shoulders. "Everyone is saying that it is certain you dye your hair!"

Now, I can tell you that I have never once dyed my hair, nor do I ever plan to do so. The problem is that someone probably looked at my hair and thought, "Dan's hair is really black and kind of shiny, so he must be dyeing his hair." However, whoever that person was didn't have all the facts. My hair is brown, but when it's wet it looks black. If I put gel or something in it, it looks black and shiny all day. Luckily this rumor didn't cause me any pain, and I can easily laugh about it.

Unfortunately, gossip is usually done with the intent to harm someone else. Shared information about someone else's life almost always seems to be negative. An unjustified rumor is a dangerous thing.

My wife has a piece she cut out of the newspaper called "Nobody's Friend" (author unknown). It reads like this:

> My name is Gossip. I have no respect for justice. I maim without killing. I break hearts and ruin lives. I am cunning and malicious and gather strength with age. The more I am quoted the more I am believed. My victims are

helpless. They cannot protect themselves against me because I have no name or face. To track me down is impossible. The harder you try the more elusive I become. I am nobody's friend. Once I tarnish a reputation it is never the same. I topple governments and wreck marriages. I ruin careers and cause sleepless nights, heartaches and indigestion. I make innocent people cry in their pillows. Even my name hisses. I am called 'Gossip.' I make headlines and headaches.

That is why James is warning us about the tongue and our words that can start a fire that begins so small and grows so fast.

## Fire Hurts People

We all saw the specials on 9/11 and watched the huge flames coming from the Twin Towers. Many people leaped from the burning buildings, falling to the ground to certain death. It was a horrible situation.

Our bodies naturally want to avoid intense heat. That's why those people preferred to jump from a hundred-story building and be killed instantly rather than stay and wait for the flames to consume them. We don't want to be near anything that is very hot; fire hurts!

Another word that comes to mind when we think of hurtful speech is *slander*, which is defined by Webster as "the utterance of false charges or misrepresentations which defame and damage another's reputation."[2] If we are slandering someone, our intent from the very beginning is to do damage. We want to cause them pain and ruin his or her reputation. We are all familiar with political campaigns that slander opponents, trying to bring them down by questioning their integrity.

The Bible uses different words for *slander* like *evil speaking* (KJV), *strife*, and *destruction*. One of the Ten Commandments is, "You shall not give false testimony against your neighbor" (Exodus 20:16).

A few years ago, I spent some time in Portland, Oregon, with a friend of mine whom I had worked with at the Luis Palau

Evangelistic Association. As we got together for lunch, I asked Gil how his church was doing. He had started the church about seven years earlier on the east side of Portland, and it had grown rapidly to more than three hundred people. I was shocked at his response: "We had a burial service for the church."

He explained that some people had come from another church, and it was like taking in poison. These new people had gotten into various ministries, and their negativity had caused the old members to start leaving the church rapidly. Attendance continued to drop until there were fewer than a hundred people left. So Gil held one final celebration service, and then closed the church. He told me that the gossiping and slandering had gotten so bad, and so many people had been driven away by it, that it was not worth sticking it out any longer. The fire that had spread through his church had hurt many, many people and had eventually killed the church itself.

## Fire Leaves Its Signature

You have probably seen buildings that have recently burned down or a forest that has recently been scorched. You can smell the destruction.

I was in Connecticut for an event; our chairman had experienced a house fire that had begun in the chimney. He asked me if I would come over and pray with his family for the house. It was two weeks after the fire when I walked into his house. I couldn't stay in there. The smoke damage was incredible. The smoke had soaked into everything—the walls, the carpet, the paint, and the furniture. I don't know if they were ever able to move back. Fire leaves a permanent mark and a lasting smell.

Pastors will often come into a new church and smell the lingering smoke of past fires. It doesn't take long before they know something isn't right. This family won't talk to that family. If this person is involved, that person won't be involved. When a name is mentioned, people wince or roll their eyes. It may have started ten or twenty years ago, but the new pastor can still smell the lingering effects of that fire. He can see the lasting consequences of gossip and slander.

James is saying to this relatively new church, "The mouth, the tongue, the words, are like a fire. It starts small, grows fast, burns people up, and leaves its signature. We've got to stop it."

## The Invisible Killer

In an old movie called *The Mechanic*, actors Charles Bronson and Jan-Michael Vincent play a pair of hired assassins. Neither one trusts the other because they both know the art of assassination and all the various ways to kill the other person.

At the end of the movie, they celebrate because they have pulled off the job they were hired to do and have received their money. They have a bottle of wine, and Bronson takes a drink. Immediately, he knows that something is wrong. As he stumbles around and falls over the furniture, Vincent tells him what kind of poison he put into the glass so that Bronson could not smell it or see it. Bronson dies, and Vincent excitedly grabs the money and races out to the car. As he jumps in, he spots a note hanging from the mirror that says, "If you are reading this note, it means I'm dead. So are you." Boom! The movie ends. They didn't trust each other for good reason.

The poison was invisible, but it did incredible damage. In his second analogy, James compares the tongue to poison (that is, salt water, see verse 11). We often don't know where rumors start, but we do know they do quite a bit of damage. Poison can also be slow acting. It can get into our systems and slowly eat away at us. We may have gone through verbal abuse or a lack of affection that has slowly poisoned our lives. On the other hand, we have all known people who have encouraged us at one time or another. A word of affirmation or affection can be just as powerful as a word of gossip or slander.

James reminds us that the same tongue we use to praise God is also used to curse men. This shouldn't be! A salt spring shouldn't produce fresh water, nor should a tree produce fruit of a different kind. Instead of using our tongues for good, too often we are starting fires and spewing out poison all over the place. That is not the way it should work! We should be lifting people up and encouraging them. We should use our tongues the way God intended.

We don't encourage nearly as often as we should. We need to be so filled with the Spirit of God that it just comes naturally to us to affirm people, to thank them, and to lift them up. We have the power to discourage and destroy, and we have the power to encourage and edify.

Sticks and stones didn't break my bones as a child, but words certainly hurt me.

Remember, what comes out of our mouths is what is in our hearts. May we guard our hearts and ask God to fill them with his love and his mercy so that we treat people the way they should be treated: as his children.

Worldly wisdom
evaluates everything
by the standards of
this world and
society, not by what
the Bible says.

## CHAPTER 18

# THE DANGERS OF WORLDLY WISDOM

*JAMES 3:13–16*

Two Texans are bragging to each other about the sizes of their ranches. One asks the other, "What's the name of your ranch anyway?"

"Well," the other rancher draws a deep breath. "It's The Rocking R, Flying W, Circle C, Bar U, Staple 4, Rolling M, Rainbow's End, ABC, Silver Spur Ranch."

"Wow!" the other man says. "So how many cattle do you have?"

"Not that many. Most of them don't live through the branding."

This man was smart enough to have a big ranch, but not very wise in running it. He was killing off his cattle just trying to put the mark on their hindquarters.

In this passage, James moves from talking about how we speak to one another to how we live with one another. He also speaks about the wisdom we display. There are two kinds of wisdom in these verses; in this chapter, we will deal with worldly wisdom.

## The Origin of Worldly Wisdom

Wisdom is the art of applying knowledge. It is taking knowledge, the things that we know, and applying it to our lives to make them better, to bring them more in line with what the Lord wants us to be, and how he wants us to act.

The early church was having some problems. James knew that they were not acting the way Jesus had taught. He pointed to worldly wisdom as the root of the problem. In verse 14 he tells them, "But if you harbor bitter envy and selfish ambition in your hearts, do not boast about it or deny the truth." Worldly wisdom begins and ends with human beings. It is something that originates with us. It doesn't seek God for his wisdom, for his thoughts, for his direction. Worldly wisdom is the kind of wisdom that comes from acquiring the knowledge of this world.

Heraclitus, the Greek philosopher, said, "The abundance of knowledge does not teach men to be wise."[1] Many people think they are very intelligent, and they may be by the world's standards of wisdom. In our society, we tend to worship knowledge. Even in our conversations, we don't really listen to what others are saying. We are always waiting for the moment when we can interject our own opinions, so they can see how smart and how well informed we are.

Many people who think they are intelligent have been quite disappointed. Thomas Watson, the chairman of IBM in 1943, said, "I think there is a world market for maybe five computers."[2] Today, some people have five computers in one house. In 1977, Ken Olson, founder and president of Digital Equipment Corporation, said, "There is no reason anyone would want a computer in their home."[3] These men thought they were pretty smart, and they were, but they were also dead wrong.

The interesting thing about worldly wisdom, and those who think they have it, is the fact that, for many of them, their lives are a mess. It seems to me that they have knowledge, and they can stand on a podium and give information, but they can't take information and make it work in their daily lives with real people, real relationships, and real problems.

This happens in the Christian world as well. I had two professors in college who were very intelligent, but they had a sense of pride and arrogance about them. They could talk for hours on end, and tell others everything they may have ever wanted to know about the Bible. They had all kinds of biblical knowledge and received great recognition, but they didn't know how to apply it to their lives. They both ended up committing adultery, and their ministries were destroyed.

Benjamin Franklin wrote, "He that falls in love with himself will have no rivals."[4] It is very true. So much of worldly wisdom comes from self-love.

## How Worldly Wisdom Operates

In verse 16 James says, "For where you have envy and selfish ambition, there you find disorder and every evil practice." Worldly wisdom operates in a place of envy or jealousy. It is a selfish zeal. Worldly wisdom comes from pure selfishness. It is concerned with attaining, with pushing forward in life. Worldly wisdom evaluates everything by the standards of this world and society, not by what the Bible says.

So if we are motivated by worldly wisdom, what are we envying? For one thing, we are envious of other people's positions. I love that line from Bette Midler, the actress/singer, "The worst part of success is to try to find someone who is happy for you."[5] That is so true. We tell other people, "I'm so happy for you. I think it's great what you have accomplished," but in our hearts, we are envious of that person's position.

Joseph and his brothers are a great biblical example. Joseph's brothers were envious of his favored position in the eyes of their father. Their worldly wisdom was telling them, "Why should he be above us? He's younger anyway. Let's just get rid of him" (see Genesis 37:1–19).

We are also envious of other people's possessions. Someone else always has the newer, bigger, updated, and better version of the things we desire. That's what advertising is based on: jealousy and envy. Manufacturers tell us, "You need to have this product because everyone else is getting it." We buy into that worldly wisdom, which is based on those same human traits.

Sometimes we are also jealous and envious of other people's personalities. No matter how popular or respected we may be, there is always that one person who walks into a room and lights it up, attracting everyone's attention. We wish that he or she wasn't there, taking the spotlight off us. That is the jealousy of worldly wisdom. We are also envious of other people's power, abilities, and influence.

Jesus taught exactly the opposite. In Luke 9:23, he said, "If anyone would come after me, he must deny himself and take up his cross daily and follow me." He doesn't want us buying into the worldly wisdom of jealousy, envy, greed, and selfishness that comes across through our TVs and radios, our print media, and our shopping malls. Nothing in our society tells us to deny ourselves as Jesus taught.

The wisdom of our society says, "More is better." The plan of our materialistic society is, "Work hard, accumulate, retire at fifty-five, and then have a great time." As Americans, we have more stuff in our garages than most people in this world will have in their lifetimes. Our garbage disposals probably eat better than one-third of the people in the world.

I recently received a royalty check in the mail for some book sales. The first thing that came to my mind was, "What kind of Harley equipment can I get with this?" I had the parts all picked out, and in my head, I had already spent the money.

Then the Holy Spirit reminded me of a letter I had received earlier that week. It was from a man in Southern California regarding the pastors' conference I was preparing to hold in Nairobi, Kenya. In it he said, "The Lord laid on my heart that I should give two hundred dollars to support the pastors at your conference. My wife and I have been praying about it, and I just received my paycheck, which, due to some overtime, is exactly two hundred dollars more than I was expecting. You will find the money enclosed with this letter."

I showed the letter to my wife, and it brought great joy to both of us. How could I now be thinking of spending all the extra money I had received on things for myself? I get upset with myself at times because I think like the world. I get a little extra money and I think, "Ah ha, what can I do with this windfall? What can I buy?" Instead, I should be thinking: "Lord, what do you want me to do with this extra money? How do you want me to deny myself? How do you want me to spend this money to further your kingdom and bring joy to someone else?"

There is a cost to following Jesus. He did not teach us to give just so we would have a theoretical, abstract idea to follow. Christianity is a reality, a way of life. I often think, "What will it be like when I stand before God in heaven, and he looks at my life, at what I did and how I used my resources?"

In Christian ministry, we love to see people who have a zeal for the Lord, a brother or sister who is really serving him joyfully and wholeheartedly. Unfortunately, the problem with zeal is that sometimes it is hidden behind phrases like, "God told me to," or "I just felt led."

When I came to the Lord, I began to read the biographies of great Christian leaders and missionaries, and I was awed by their lives and ministries. I thought, "Lord, these people loved you more than I could ever love you." The older I got, however, the more I realized that we all face the demon of self. I began to realize that a little green monster of envy made me want to say, "God put it on my heart," when what I was really doing was something totally selfish.

How can we tell the difference between zeal and selfish ambition? There is a very fine line between "I'm doing this for the Lord" and "I'm doing this for myself." That line can be so fine that sometimes we can't even tell when we have crossed it. That's why I think we will all be surprised by the rewards we receive when we get to heaven. One person may say, "Lord, all I did was give someone a cup of cold water," but the Lord will reward him because his motives were pure. Another may say, "Lord, I gave away thousands of dollars," but he will not be rewarded because his giving was purely selfish; he was only thinking about himself.

I have found that when we do something out of selfish ambition, envy, or jealousy, God intervenes against us. We have to be careful of the worldly wisdom that says, "It's all about me." To each of us Jesus says, "Deny yourself, take up your cross, and follow me."

## Outcome of Worldly Wisdom

I read a news article about a woman who lived in a big-city neighborhood that was quickly going downhill. It was becoming overcrowded and dirty, and there were people there who were up to no good. She wanted to do something to help fix the situation, but she knew that she would need money and resources.

The woman started a fund-raising drive to solicit the money needed to improve the situation. She called people and sent letters to various foundations asking them to help her with her cause. She raised eighty-five thousand dollars for her project. Then she took the money and used it to move out of the neighborhood and buy herself a better home.

What happens when we are filled with worldly wisdom? James says, "For where you have envy and selfish ambition, there you find disorder and every evil practice" (3:16). This woman had plenty of worldly wisdom.

The word *disorder* in this verse literally means "restlessness" and "unsettledness"—and we definitely have disorder in our society! Out of this disorder, we have evil practices, or worthless activities and deeds that are good for nothing. They have no benefit whatsoever.

You may be in a situation in life in which worldly wisdom has influenced you to buy into a lie, and now you need some of God's wisdom. If so, go to him and say, "Lord, fill me with the wisdom that I need to make my life meaningful, to make my life count for your kingdom, to make my life count for what you want me to do."

The Bible tells us that God created each one of us for a specific purpose. He gave each one of us gifts to use for him (Ephesians 2:10; 1 Corinthians 12:7). Are we using those gifts? God didn't save and redeem us so that we could live on earth to accumulate stuff and say, "Isn't life great?" That is not why he saved us.

We may be smart, we may have a lot of knowledge, but it won't do us any good if we do not know how to apply it to our lives. I pray that God will give us the heavenly wisdom to know how to use the knowledge he has given, so that we may further his work and live the way he wants us to live.

## CHAPTER 19

# GOD'S WISDOM IN ACTION

## JAMES 3:17–18

U sually when parents have their first baby, they are extremely careful and protective of him. If he drops his pacifier on the floor, they immediately pick it up and sterilize it. For the second child, however, they pick it up, wipe it off, and stick it back in the baby's mouth. By the time the third child comes along and drops the pacifier, they tell the dog to "Fetch!"

When their first toddler swallows a coin, new parents immediately rush to the emergency room and demand X-rays. Once they have the second child, they patiently wait for the coin to pass. With the third kid, they just deduct the coin from his allowance. Most parents relax as time goes on and as they gain more wisdom in parenting.

In these verses, James moves from his discussion of worldly wisdom to godly wisdom. In the Bible, godly wisdom is described as precious, and we are instructed to seek after it (see Proverbs 4:7; 8:11).

## Why We Need Wisdom

I remember the first time I joined a parachurch organization (a ministry that comes alongside of the church to help the church). The first week I worked at the organization, I got in trouble. I was standing out in the hallway chatting, and the executive director came and asked me into his office. He said bluntly, "This is not a church, and you are not a youth pastor, so don't act like one." In other words, he was telling me that this was a corporation, a business, and although we did ministry, it was quite different from that of a local church. We didn't take company time to help people with problems. We had to be exact about lunch breaks, and we had to fill out the piles of forms requested by the business office.

I learned to adjust to the way the parachurch organization operated. When I started Eternity Minded Ministries, I had a good grasp of the way this type of organization should run.

Then God called me to pastor a church near San Francisco, California. One of my biggest struggles has been leading and managing a church that is so different from the parachurch structure to which I have become accustomed. In many ways, the chain of command is much more difficult to see, because everyone is involved—the staff, the elders, and the people. Everyone has his or her own opinions, preferences, and pet peeves.

This passage in James means so much to me personally, because I find myself in great need of God's wisdom. I have a great burden, because I want to be a good leader of my congregation, yet I have to try to maintain a delicate balance between managing the ministry and keeping my friendships intact. The decisions I make affect everyone, and everyone else's decisions affect me.

As I studied these verses, I felt an incredible burden, and I just said, "God, I truly need your wisdom." Sometimes we say that glibly—too often it has become somewhat of a canned response. But there are times when we sincerely cry out before the Lord, "God, without your wisdom, I just don't know what to do. I don't know which way to turn." We all need wisdom, and I can attest to that fact in my own life. Thankfully, God hears our cries for help.

## What God's Wisdom Is Like

"But the wisdom that comes from heaven is first of all pure; then peace-loving, considerate, submissive, full of mercy and good fruit, impartial and sincere" (3:17).

James very clearly describes the characteristics of God's wisdom. The early church at this time had a spirit of contention, bitterness, fighting, and worldly wisdom. James wanted to show his readers a better way.

The first, basic characteristic of heavenly wisdom is purity. The wisdom that comes from God has pure motives. It is the opposite of selfish ambition. In Colossians 3:23–24 the apostle Paul wrote, "Whatever you do, work at it with all your heart, as working for the Lord, not for men, since you know that you will receive an inheritance from the Lord as a reward. It is the Lord Christ you are serving." Whether we are teaching a class, serving on a board, singing in a worship team, working with toddlers, or going on a mission trip to Africa, it should be because we want to serve the Lord. The motivation for what we do and the decisions we make should be pure.

Second, heavenly wisdom is peace-loving. A sign on a church door read, "The peacemaking meeting scheduled for today has been cancelled due to a conflict." We all have conflicts. We have them in our families, in our friendships, within the church, and at our workplaces. However, wisdom produces peace. In this passage, James is saying to us, "Do you know how you're going to figure out if you have the wisdom of God in your church? There is going to be a spirit of peace, not one of contentiousness and quarreling."

The word James uses for *peace-loving* here actually means "to bind or weave together." It doesn't mean "peace no matter the cost"; at times there must be confrontation. Sometimes we may have to go to a brother or sister in a spirit of love and say, "I see something in your life, and it's not right." But this is the kind of peace that keeps us from demanding our rights and from being overly critical with other people. Godly wisdom is peace-loving, not self-seeking.

The third characteristic of God's wisdom is that it is considerate. Some translations say *gentle*. This is a hard word to translate, and scholars have struggled with it. It carries the idea of not treating people with harshness. A considerate person is not mean-spirited or withdrawn. It is a person who wants to reach out with gentleness to those who do not know Jesus.

I have heard Christians say things like, "I really told that person off," speaking of their encounter with someone at a store or a gas station. Sadly, our interactions with the world are not always carried out in a spirit of gentleness. James says that godly wisdom is pure, peace-loving, and considerate (or gentle) in the way we deal with people outside of the church as well as within the body of believers.

Next, in describing godly wisdom James uses a word we don't often like to hear—*submissive*. It means that we should be approachable to one another. We should not be walking around with a chip on our shoulders, ready to pick a fight. To be submissive is to be compliant and willing to change, willing to say, "I was wrong in that situation; I'm sorry." The submissive person doesn't say, "I want my way, and I'm going to get it, no matter what anyone else thinks."

A man was telling his friend about a new hearing aid. "It's great," he said. "It cost me four thousand dollars, and it is state of the art."

His friend asked, "What kind is it?"

The man looked at his watch and replied, "Twelve thirty."

Sometimes the things that we think are working great really are not. The spirit of the submissive person says, "Let's be reasonable. Let's be open. If it doesn't work, let's try something different."

Next, James says that godly wisdom is full of mercy and good fruit (see Galatians 6:22–23). The mercy James is speaking of here refers to feelings of pity, compassion, and kindness, toward both the saint and the sinner. Showing mercy in a helpful, practical way should be our natural reaction to the mercy we have been shown by God (see Luke 6:36).

The sixth quality of God's wisdom is harder than it sounds. Being impartial in our treatment of others is not natural. James has already talked about the way the early church was showing favoritism to the rich. We tend to show extra grace toward those who have something we would like to get. When it comes to making decisions, we can be tempted to favor those whose money or goodwill we most desire. But this is not the way that a person full of God's wisdom should operate.

Finally, this heavenly wisdom is sincere. It is free from hypocrisy; it doesn't pretend to be something it is not. As Christians, we should be people who are characterized by honesty and truthfulness. God does not want lip service from us. Some believers have an appearance of goodness in their actions and in the way they treat others, but they lack the sincerity and authenticity that should distinguish true followers of Christ.

James says that as we work, minister, and worship together, these things should be the mark of the church that is using and exercising heavenly wisdom.

## Now Let's Live It!

We hear a lot about change. Some people want it; others despise it. Change can be a hard thing. We make good changes, and we make bad changes, and we often have to go back and evaluate whether we made the right decisions in those changes.

The change God is interested in, however, is the change that affects our hearts. He is concerned with the kind of change that motivates us to come to him, drop to our knees in brokenness, and lift up our hands to him in worship and praise. He is looking for the change that causes us to ask ourselves: "Are my life and my faith real?"

I recently received a very encouraging letter from a man named Gary. It is so relevant to this subject that I would like to share it with you:

> Dear Dan, I've just returned from a three-week trip to Kursk, Russia, a city of about 500,000 people. The day I left, I had a struggle about whether or not I should take your books with me. I later understood that the struggle that was taking place in my mind was a spiritual one, as God wanted to speak to me through your books, and Satan did not want me to hear the message. I've been a Christian for eighteen years, but there was one big area in my life that I was unwilling to give to the Lord.
>
> Well, my friend, God convicted me right there in

Russia, 7,800 miles away from home, that he wanted all of my heart, not just part of it. I began to weep. I began to confess my sin, my pride, and my lack of faith in the Lord. Just as Peter had failed the Lord and denied Jesus, I too had been denying a part of my life to the Lord. But Jesus treated me just like he responded to Peter. He didn't push me or chastise me. He just loved me. What a delight to walk in obedience to the Lord.

Dan, other than my salvation eighteen years ago, this was the most exciting and spiritually profitable time in my life. Was it because of your books? No. It was because I listened to the Holy Spirit and asked the Lord with all sincerity to have his way with me, to break me, and mold me. What a deliverance, and what a Savior.

Dan, thank you so much for listening to the prompting of your heart in writing the books.

In his mighty love, your brother in Christ, Gary.

That kind of work only comes through prayer, through fasting, and through being honest before God. It is my prayer that God will give you and me his wisdom and that he will allow us to be people who hear his voice. Only he can help us give up those areas in our lives where we have been using worldly wisdom, and not his wisdom.

Back in chapter 1, James told us, "If any of you lacks wisdom, he should ask God, who gives generously to all without finding fault, and it will be given to him" (1:5). May God give us his wisdom, and may he teach us humility, honesty, and transparency so that we can be real, not only with him but also with one another.

## CHAPTER 20

# A CALL TO CEASE FIRE

*JAMES 4:1–12*

Someone has said, "Peace is that brief glorious moment in history when everybody stands around reloading."

Sometimes peace is hard to come by. After World War II, the United Nations was formed with one goal. The goal was to assure that succeeding generations would be free from the scourge of war. Since that time, there has not been a moment when there has not been warfare going on some place in the world.

According to the *Personnel Journal*, from the beginning of recorded history 3,530 years ago, the entire world has been at peace in 286 of those years—only 8 percent of the time. It is also estimated that during that same time period more than eight thousand treaties have been made—and broken.[1]

We really are a people of war. When we travel to other places, especially third-world countries, we see how true this statement is. We can pick up the newspaper in the morning and read about a war going on somewhere nearly every day. We live in a world at war.

I don't think it will get much better until Jesus comes back. In Isaiah 9:6 he is called the Prince of Peace, but until he comes, the Bible clearly teaches that things will go from bad to worse no matter how many treaties are signed, no matter how many cease-fires are declared (Matthew 24:6; 2 Timothy 3:1–5). Peace is a hard thing to come by.

We are also at war on a personal level. These verses in James are not "feel good" passages. In them James is dealing with heavy topics—warfare and fighting.

## We Are at War with Each Other

In verse 1, James asks the question, "What causes fights and quarrels among you?" In this verse he uses these two words, one meaning a spontaneous fight, the other a chronic state of warfare—quarreling. He loves these people, and he is genuinely concerned about them. Therefore, he wants to know what is causing so much unrest among them.

A magazine called *The Door* (formerly *The Wittenberg Door*) offers a brutal and often honest satire of the church. On the front cover of the first issue I ever picked up, there was a picture of church steps, with a pastor and some elders or deacons standing around smiling. I thought, "What could be so bad about that?"

I flipped through the magazine, skimming a few articles, then turned it over to look at the back. There I found quite a different picture. Whereas the front cover had shown the front of these men, the back cover showed their backs. One had a knife sticking in the other man's back. Another man was picking a wallet out of another guy's pocket. One man had a copy of *Playboy* magazine hanging out of his back pocket. The picture looked good on the front cover, but what was really going on behind that scene was a totally different story.

So what were these early Christians fighting about? First, there were class wars going on among them. We read earlier about the distinction between the rich and the poor. There were those with money and those without money, and that disparity created many divisions. James knew that they were fighting among themselves because of the differences in their social classes.

Then there was war within the church. They were fighting over positions. We saw in chapter 3 that everyone wanted the honored position of a teacher or a leader. Instead of studying the Word of God and being edified, they were all trying to assert themselves by fighting over what positions they occupied. The church was being ruined by selfish ambition. Each one thought his idea was best, and nobody wanted to submit to authority.

First, the disciples of Jesus fought over who would be the greatest in the kingdom (see Mark 9:33–34). Then the early Christians argued over positions in the church (see Mark 10:35–45). As we look back over church history, we realize that this situation is not uncommon. The Corinthian church had wars going on inside of it to the point that believers were suing each other (see 1 Corinthians 3:1–23; 6:1–8). The Galatian believers were "biting and devouring each other" (see Galatians 5:15); the church at Ephesus was admonished to cultivate unity (see Ephesians 4:3); and even the great church at Philippi had a battle going on between two women that Paul had to deal with (see Philippians 4:2–3).

I imagine that James's heart was broken because of the fighting going on among these Christians. Perhaps he was thinking of the prayer of unity that Jesus prayed in John 17:20–23. Instead of being known for the love they had for one another, as Jesus had exhorted them in John 13:34–35, they were known for fighting, hatred, and discord.

We are also at war with ourselves. Verses 2 and 3 of James 4 show that wrong motives lead to wrong actions and wrong praying. We don't find this idea of denying ourselves very easy at all. So we are in a constant battle with ourselves, trying to say no to the things of the world.

## We Are at War with God

James says to these believers, "You adulterous people, don't you know that friendship with the world is hatred toward God?" (4:4). He uses the word *world* to mean society apart from God. The phrase "friendship with the world" means to be approved by the world. James is saying to these people, "Don't you understand that all this fighting, these wars, just indicate that you're really in love with this world?" He then goes on to say that to be in love with this world is to be at war with God.

Notice that James uses the word *adulterous* here. If we go back to the Old Testament, we find that God, in his dealings with Israel, would often use the marriage covenant as an illustration of his love for his people. All through the Old Testament, when Israel turned her back on God, her faithful Husband, God would come after Israel, the unfaithful wife.

James, knowing that this analogy is familiar to his readers, tells them, "You are adulteresses. By your love for the world, you are committing spiritual adultery. You are so overcommitted to society that you have turned your backs on God."

In Galatians 6:7–8 the apostle Paul wrote: "Do not be deceived: God cannot be mocked. A man reaps what he sows. The one who sows to please his sinful nature, from that nature will reap destruction; the one who sows to please the Spirit, from the Spirit will reap eternal life." When Paul talks about sowing to please the sinful nature, he means allowing the flesh to take us wherever it wants to go. When we say to the flesh, "Okay, I'll do whatever you want," when we give in to that thought or action, we are at war with God, because we are allowing the world to take his rightful place in our lives.

In this war, we are also subject to the Devil. As Charles Baudelaire, the nineteenth-century French poet, said, the greatest trick the Devil has ever played is convincing the world that he does not exist.[2] Our society scoffs and pushes the Devil aside along with his warfare, tactics, and demons. Nonetheless, he does exist. He is a liar and a deceiver, and he wants us to act in the flesh.

As Christians, you and I are targeted by the enemy. The enemy has one goal, and that goal is to separate us from God. He can't take away our salvation, but he wants us to have no prayer life, no intimacy, no walk with God, no power, and no interest in spiritual things. If he keeps us separated from God, then we are going to take our eyes away from where the real war is taking place.

A. W. Tozer wrote, "Worldliness is an accepted part of our way of life. Our religious mood is social instead of spiritual. We have lost the art of worship. We are not producing saints. Our models are successful businessmen, celebrated athletes, and theatrical personalities. We carry on our religious activities after the methods of the modern advertisers."[3] Tozer wrote those words thirty years ago, and he has been dead for some time. I wonder what he would think of us now.

As I read this passage from James, I thought, "Lord, we need a cease-fire. How can we stop these wars?"

## A New Attitude

First of all, James tells us to submit to God and resist the Devil. That word *submit* can be used as a military term, meaning to yield to authority. In other words, James is telling us, "Get under God." As soldiers of the cross, we are ordered to come under the authority of our Commander in Chief. When we are in submission to God, we will refuse to give the Devil a foothold (see Ephesians 4:27). We will resist him and say, "I'm going to be submissive to God out of love."

Knowledge of God is a far thing from love of God. We can have all the knowledge of God in the world and still not want to submit to him; but when we come to understand his love for us, we want to yield our wills to his. We can live for the world, our flesh, and the Devil, and be destroyed, or we can submit to God, who loves us as no one else can, and truly live. Why is it such a hard choice?

We don't gain knowledge from reading alone, but also from observation and experience. We can read thousands of books on automobiles, but until we actually get behind the steering wheel of a car, we will have a hard time learning to drive. For many of us, all we know of God is what we have read. We have read of his power, his omnipotence, and what he has done in the past, but we haven't observed him or experienced him personally.

In verse 8 James also tells his readers to draw near to God. He is not talking to people who have never experienced salvation. He is talking to those believers who have walked away from God. He tells them to wash their hands and purify their hearts. Then in verse 9 he tells them to stop laughing and start mourning. Of course, this doesn't mean we can't laugh and have a good time and enjoy life. James is talking about the laughter of a fool—the one who is living in sin and throwing it in God's face, saying, "I'll sin as much as I want; God will forgive me." James is saying to that person: "Don't be so stupid. Don't live that way. Repent, submit, and draw near to God, and he will draw near to you."

Finally, in verse 10 James says that we should humble ourselves before God. God hates pride. We exalt our abilities, our accomplishments, our status, and ourselves; God hates that kind of self-aggrandizement and self-worship.

In an interview with Lee Strobel, author of *The Case for Faith*, Dallas Willard said, "God ordained that people should be governed in the end by what they want."[4] God will give us what we want. If we don't want God, we don't have to have him. If we want this world and everything in it—the fights, the quarrels, the lust, the desires of the flesh—God says to us, "It's yours. You can have it." But if we say, "God, I want you. Not only do I want to know about you in my head, I also want to observe you at work in my life and to experience you in my soul," then God will show himself to us.

God has made it very clear that if we truly and earnestly seek him, we will surely find him (Hebrews 11:6). Nevertheless, we can't just say, "God, I'd like to see you work in my life, and I'd kind of like to get to know you." We have to have a passion to pursue God, to see him do miraculous things. So the question is: Do we really want to know him?

As a pastor, I go to my library each week and seek the Lord for myself and for those he has placed in my care. Sometimes when I hear from God through his Word, it is a tough passage to obey, like this one, but the outcome is well worth the effort of obeying. Who among us does not want a cease-fire in his or her soul, and to be at peace with the Master? May we be a people who resist the Devil, submit to God, draw near to him, and humble ourselves before him.

# TIME'S UP
## JAMES 4:13–17

Some children were asked about the subject of death and dying. Here are some of their responses:

> "God doesn't tell you when you are going to die because he wants it to be a big surprise." —Alan, age nine

> "You have to be old before you can die because God seems to like old people best." —Maggie, age ten

> "Doctors help you so you won't die until you pay their bills." —Stephanie, age nine

> "Only good people go to heaven; the other people go where it is hot all the time like Florida." —Judy, age eight

Some people refuse to think about death. When I traveled overseas, before I left I used to try to show my wife where all the important papers were in case something happened to me, but she wanted no part of it. Often people have experienced pain because of the death of a loved one, and now they are scared to think of their own mortality.

This passage from James has probably had a greater impact on my life than any other verses of Scripture. It really makes me stop and think. It moves me forward because I realize that my life expectancy is getting shorter every year that passes.

Lou Erickson said, "Life is like a taxi. The meter just keeps on ticking whether you are getting somewhere or just standing still."[1] That is the truth. We all have a time clock, and that clock is ticking.

Here James talks to those who are arrogant and wealthy, those who are making plans and calculating their lives without God. He says to these rich people, "You're making all these plans, but you have forgotten about God's participation in your life." James wants to remind them of a few things that are true about life.

## Life Is Complex

Whether we live in a big city, a small town, or a rural area, we are all in situations in which we deal with time, our purposes in life, a place to live, and rewards. James is talking to people who think they have all of that planned out. They are going through life without figuring God into the equation. In all their planning and making decisions, they have ignored the most important element.

In Luke 12:13–21, Jesus tells the story of the rich man who produced a good crop and thought to himself, "I have so much grain that I need bigger barns. I'll just tear down the old ones, build bigger and better ones, and then I can eat, drink, and be merry for a long time!" (He must have been an American.) God said to him, "You fool! This very night your life will be demanded from you. Then who will get what you have prepared for yourself?" (verse 20). In verse 21, Jesus said that the same is true for anyone who stores up things for himself and yet is not rich toward God.

Life is more than the abundance of our possessions (see Luke 12:15). Even in our complex lives, when we have to think about so many things, we are fools if we forget about what's going to happen at the end. If we do not allow God to be in control of our lives, they will quickly fall apart. As we deal with life, our families, and our work, how many of us look at life and ask that all-important question: "What is going to happen at the end of my life?"

One time when I was speaking in the United Kingdom, I was invited to the house of a man who had heard me the night before. I was only thirty years old at the time, and he was easily in his sixties. After everyone had left, and we were alone together, he said, "As I listened to you speak last night, something happened inside of me. You see that I have this big house. I actually have lots of homes and cars and things. But something has been missing in my life." As I talked with him about Jesus, he decided to pray and open his heart to the Lord. Afterward he said, "This is what I've been looking for all of my life."

In the complexity of his life, he had never stopped to think about God. Sometimes we are guilty of the same lack of attention and concern. We run around in a fast pace from one activity to the next, without stopping to think, "What happens at the end of my life?" In verse 14, James says that we don't even know what the next day will bring to us.

## Life Is Uncertain

I have a friend who works for the Baptist General Conference in Southern California. He and I have known each other for a few years, and we enjoy spending time together. At the age of fifty-five, he was recently diagnosed with an inoperable brain tumor. When I found out, I had just shared breakfast with him two weeks earlier, and he looked fine. Now, unless God does a miracle in his body, Avery will be with Jesus within a year or two.

Life is very uncertain. Proverbs 27:1 says, "Do not boast about tomorrow, for you do not know what a day may bring forth." In verses 13–15 of chapter 4, James really wants us to pay attention. There is no point in making a big issue over the things of this life, he is saying, when we are just passing through. We are not guaranteed any particular amount of time here.

According to James, our attitude should be, "If it is the Lord's will, we will live and do this and that" (4:15). That is not just a glib little phrase we are to use as we go right ahead and make our plans just as though our lives will go on forever. Here James is calling us to seriously understand that our lives are in the hands of God. No matter what plans we make, God numbers our days. He knows the ending; we don't.

When my family and I were living in Portland, our house was very close to a cemetery. I drove by it quite frequently, and I couldn't help but think, "One of these days my name is going to be carved on a tombstone." Although we don't really like to think about it, death is a reality—it is certain—for each of us. I can guarantee you one thing: a hundred years from now, you and I are not going to be here.

## Life Is Brief

In verse 14 James says that our lives are like a mist or a vapor that vanishes in the light of eternity. Job says, "Our days on earth are but a shadow" (Job 8:9). Death is very sudden for many people. We never know when an accident will happen.

I spoke at a winter youth retreat on Mt. Hood when I met Dave Johnson. We were having a great time skiing, but we were also having a time of great spiritual refreshment. At one point, I sat down with Dave, a seventeen-year-old who was new to the group. I asked him if he knew where he would spend eternity. He told me of his decision several months earlier to open his heart to Jesus Christ. It was a great conversation.

Two weeks later, Dave was killed when a car drifted over the center line and hit his vehicle head-on. I still have his ski equipment in my garage. I know countless stories of young people who died unexpectedly. The point is that we never know when the end will come. For some of us, it may be sooner than we think.

I have been in airplanes that have caught on fire, I have been attacked by pit bulls, I have been in riots, and I have fallen off the sides of cliffs. On more than one occasion, I have thought that my life was coming to an end. One thing I understand—when I die, I die alone. I will stand there before the Lord by myself. My mom will not be standing beside me with her arm around me saying, "Oh, God, you've got to let Danny in. He was a great little boy." It will be between God and me.

Some day each of us must face God and give an account of our life. So why do we live as though nothing is ever going to happen to us? Why do we make plans for the future, giving no thought to God? Why do we continue as if we are going to be here forever?

When I was in seminary, I had to take a class called "Death and Dying." It wasn't exactly a cheerful class, but it was very helpful.

We read a book called *Beyond Death's Door* by Dr. Maurice Rawlings,[2] a cardiologist and professor of medicine at the University of Tennessee. He wrote about his experiences with patients as they transitioned into eternity.

Several years after his book was published, I read an article in *OMNI* magazine, in which he wrote, "Just listening to these patients has changed my whole life. There is a life after death and if I don't know where I'm going it's not safe to die."[3]

In this passage, James is saying, "You shouldn't brag; you shouldn't boast. You shouldn't be making all these plans. You should be thinking about the fact that your life here is brief, and that your relationship with God is more important than the activities you engage in and things you do in this life."

In the youth group I worked with at Cedar Mill Bible Church in Portland, there was a fifteen-year-old girl named Stephanie who had a bubbly personality and an energetic smile. She was the only child of her parents, who were both active in our church.

One day Stephanie wasn't feeling well, so her mom picked her up from school. They went to the doctor and later found out that she had leukemia. The doctors immediately began chemotherapy treatments. Stephanie soon lost her hair and had to wear a wig, dropped out of school for a while, and gave up a lot of activities she had enjoyed doing, yet she maintained a positive attitude. Our church rallied around her to support and encourage her.

After a while, the leukemia went into remission, and we had a tremendous feeling of hope. She went back to school, and life was normal for a while. Then one day the leukemia came back. Within a few days, her mom called me and asked me to come down to the hospital to pray with Stephanie. She was in a coma, but they thought she could still hear. I was only twenty-eight at the time, and there I was with this sixteen-year-old girl who was lying on the bed with tubes and wires everywhere, convulsing because her fever was so high.

I sat down beside her bed and began to read Psalm 23. I got about halfway through it and began crying. I knew this girl was not going to be around much longer. I closed my Bible and whispered in her ear, "Stephanie, one of these days, I'm going to see you in heaven."

I walked back out to her parents; I could see in their faces that they knew they were losing their only child. I asked her mom, "Did Stephanie have any idea that she was turning for the worse?"

Her mom told me that the previous afternoon, Stephanie had called her parents to her room and said, "Mom and Dad, tomorrow I'm going to die, but don't worry about me. I'm going to be with Jesus." She passed away the next day. At sixteen years of age, she stared death in the face with more confidence than most of us adults have about going to meet our Maker.

Why are we so wrapped up in the complexity of life? The important thing is not what we do, but who we become. Eventually, our lives will end, and then what will matter is whether or not we knew Jesus as Savior.

In light of eternity, our lives are very brief. They are also uncertain—we never know when God will call us home. But for those of us who have trusted in Christ as Savior, we do not need to fear death. We have a blessed hope that when our time on earth is up, we have a perfect heavenly home.

Do you have that blessed hope? Do you have the certainty that Stephanie had? If not, you can pray right now and ask Jesus Christ to come into your life and give you the hope of eternity.

## CHAPTER 22

# IT'S A FACT: MONEY TALKS

## JAMES 5:1–6

Aminister receives a telephone call from a distressed woman whose cat has just died. She asks the minister if he will perform a funeral for her dead cat, Homer. The man thinks about it for a minute, and then says that he doesn't think it would fit his job description as a Baptist minister. He tells her about the Presbyterian minister down the road who might do it.

The woman is a bit frustrated, but she calls the Presbyterian minister. He explains apologetically that his board would probably not give him permission to hold a funeral for Homer. Finally, she calls the Methodist minister, but he says that he cannot do it either. He suggests she call the Baptist minister again.

She calls the Baptist minister back, and this time she says, "I've checked with the other ministers, and they won't hold a funeral for Homer. I really want my cat buried properly, so I've decided to give a thousand dollars to the minister who will do a funeral for my cat. I'd really prefer that you do it because I'm a Baptist too."

The minister thinks about it for a second, then he answers, "Well, you should have told me from the beginning that your cat was Baptist. Of course I'll do the funeral."

Money certainly has a way of changing things. I have been in situations in which I am invited to speak somewhere, and I really don't want to miss an activity with my family, or be away for the weekend. As I start to say I am not interested, those familiar little words come up, "What would it take to get you here for the week-end?" It reflects our belief that money talks.

As I read this passage, I thought, *Who in the world is James talking to? I've got wealth. Am I in trouble now? Is misery coming to me?*

James may have had some wealthy people in his audience. Perhaps he knew some rich people who would be visiting the churches where this letter was read. I am not exactly sure, but I do know that his tone has changed. He doesn't start off the way he does in some of his paragraphs with, "Listen, brothers." In verse 1 of this passage he says, "Now listen, you rich people," and then just goes after them.

At the time James wrote these words, a person's status depended on the amount of land that individual owned. James was probably addressing some of the wealthy landowners of his day. These people lived by the Golden Rule: He who has the gold makes the rules. Let me give you some thoughts as to why James wrote this passage. Let's talk about money, because money does speak. Money tells us about what we value, what we hold dear, what is important in our lives. Money talks about our heart.

## Money Reveals Our Priorities

James must have been thinking about the story in Luke chapter 12 of the rich man who had a huge crop of grain and decided to build bigger barns so he could "kick back and relax." In verse 3 of chapter 5 James says, "You have hoarded wealth in the last days." He must have remembered what Jesus said about the person who hoards money and thinks of no one but himself.

I see three problems with hoarding. First, it is usually done because of the desire for selfish pleasure. Does the Lord want us to work and earn a living? Does the Lord want us to have food and clothing? Of course. Yet, God opposes excess accumulation for the purpose of selfish pleasure.

The second problem with hoarding is that it provides a false sense of security. I have a savings account, and I like having it. God is not opposed to saving. But God doesn't like it when we rely on our savings as the means to bail us out of trouble, when we put our trust in our savings instead of in him.

The final problem with hoarding is that it takes money away from those who need it most. This is the case for the people to whom James was writing. The poor laborers were not getting enough to live on because the wealthy were hoarding it all.

We must understand the difference between hoarding and saving. God certainly does not intend for us to be lazy. In 1 Timothy 5:8 Paul wrote, "If anyone does not provide for his relatives, and especially for his immediate family, he has denied the faith and is worse than an unbeliever." We are definitely supposed to work, earn money, and support our families. Working and saving are both important.

In the parable of the talents in Matthew 25:14–30, a master calls his servants to give an account of the funds he entrusted to them before he left on a journey. The first two have been productive with their master's wealth in his absence, but the third one has done nothing with it but hide it. To this unproductive servant the master says, "You should have put my money on deposit with the bankers, so that when I returned I would have received it back with interest" (verse 27). The Bible says a lot about money and saving and taking care of family. However, the Bible also warns us about hoarding.

Another word for hoarding is *greed*. Sometimes we know there is greed in our lives, but at other times we don't even recognize it.

When I was offered a position as pastor at Fair Oaks Baptist Church, the elders told me that they would give me a certain amount of money as a salary. They also told me that they would give me some money to help with the process of moving and buying a house. I gratefully received the money as I started into that ministry.

One day it dawned on me that I didn't need all the money I had been given. I could have bought my house with less money. As I saw that the church was struggling a little bit financially, I realized that I had been wrong to tuck that extra money away when I didn't really need it. I talked to my wife about it, and we agreed that we should give back half of the money we had been given to buy our house. It just hit me how greedy I had been in hoarding that money for myself.

James is telling us that hoarding is not a healthy thing and that how we use the money God has given us speaks volumes about our priorities. Money also tells us whether we are honest or dishonest with what we have been given.

## Money Reveals Our Practices

A woman was lying on a beach in Florida, soaking up some sun. A little boy walked up to her rather abruptly and said, "Ma'am, do you believe in God?"

The woman was a bit taken aback, but she answered, "Yes, I believe in God."

"Do you go to church and read the Bible and pray every day?" the little boy asked.

The woman looked at him curiously. "Yes, I do."

"Great!" he said. "Will you hold my quarter for me while I go swimming?" That little boy knew what kind of person could be trusted with money.

These rich landowners whom James is talking about were going out and hiring laborers to work their fields, then at the end of the day, they wouldn't pay them. In Deuteronomy 24:14–15, God commanded the Israelites, "Do not take advantage of a hired man who is poor and needy, whether he is a brother Israelite or an alien living in one of your towns. Pay him his wages each day before sunset, because he is poor and is counting on it." The Bible is so practical. These laborers didn't have money stored up for a rainy day. They needed the money they earned each day to buy food for their families.

Proverbs 13:11 says, "Dishonest money dwindles away, but he who gathers money little by little makes it grow." You and I may say, "I'm not dishonest. I pay my bills." But there is another issue. We can be dishonest simply by not giving back to God what really belongs to him. God has not just suggested that we give to him—he has absolutely commanded it (see Malachi 3:8–12).

We can say, "Lord, I'm going through a hard time right now."

We can make all kinds of excuses. But God is the one who has given us the air we breathe, the hearts that are beating inside of us, our health and our jobs, and he wants us to recognize that fact. Giving is an act of worship and appreciation. It is not about paying a legalistic tithe, it is about giving out of a grateful heart to God.

It's not easy to think, "How much more can I give? How much less can I live on?" Life is expensive, and we all go through tough times financially. The problem is that we don't give God the opportunity to prove himself, as he tells us to do in Malachi 3:10. Why not pay God first and let him work? It's not as though God is oblivious to our financial conditions. We need to say, "God, I've got all these bills, and I don't know what I'm going to do, but I'm going to write the first check to you." Money definitely reveals not only our priorities but also our practices.

James knows that most of his audience is poor. They are looking at the wealthy people of their community and thinking, *Wouldn't it be great to be like them?* James knew the danger of envy. He also knew the judgment that was coming to these wealthy people because they were taking advantage of the poor. He didn't want Christians to be caught up in wishing for the life of the wealthy, because it was going to come to ruin.

Right now you may be going through some hard financial times. You may be feeling envious of those unbelievers around you who seem to have everything going for them. Listen to these words from the psalmist:

> But as for me, my feet had almost slipped; I had nearly lost my foothold. For I envied the arrogant when I saw the prosperity of the wicked. They have no struggles; their bodies are healthy and strong. They are free from the burdens common to man; they are not plagued by human ills. Therefore pride is their necklace; they clothe themselves with violence. From their callous hearts comes iniquity; the evil conceits of their minds know no limits. They scoff, and speak with malice; in their arrogance they threaten oppression.... This is what the wicked are like—always carefree,

they increase in wealth. Surely in vain have I kept my heart pure; in vain have I washed my hands in innocence. All day long I have been plagued; I have been punished every morning. (Psalm 73:2–8, 12–14)

The psalmist is writing from his heart. He is saying, "Lord, I've been watching these wealthy people, and their lives look great. I've followed you, but I have all these problems." Then in verses 18 through 26 he realizes what is going to happen to these people he envies so much:

Surely you place them on slippery ground; you cast them down to ruin.

How suddenly are they destroyed, completely swept away by terrors! As a dream when one awakes, so when you arise, O Lord, you will despise them as fantasies. When my heart was grieved and my spirit embittered, I was senseless and ignorant; I was a brute beast before you. Yet I am always with you; you hold me by my right hand. You guide me with your counsel, and afterward you will take me into glory. Whom have I in heaven but you? And earth has nothing I desire besides you. My flesh and my heart may fail, but God is the strength of my heart and my portion forever.

James wanted to remind his readers that they had more than all the rich people combined—they had God and the hope of heaven. What more could they ask?

I pray that we will be encouraged by that thought. Let us give generously, out of a thankful heart, not hoarding our money like wealthy fools. God is looking at our hearts.

James reminds us in a practical way that life is a vapor, here for a short time and then gone. Money tells about our lives on earth, but once we get to heaven, it won't matter how much money we had or didn't have. What will matter is how we used the money and resources with which God has so richly blessed us.

## CHAPTER 23

# GOD CALLS US TO ENDURANCE

### JAMES 5:7–12

A man is sitting in his car at an intersection. The traffic light is green, but he doesn't move. The people in the cars lined up behind him begin honking. He still doesn't move. The honking increases. The man becomes very frustrated by all the honking. He gets out of his car and walks to the one behind him. The driver rolls down his window, and the man says, "I'm sorry, I can't seem to get my car started, but if you'd like, you can go try to start it, and I'll sit in your car and honk the horn at you."

We are not a very patient society. In chapter 1, James talked about patience or perseverance in the light of trials. Here in chapter 5 he discusses patience again, but this time it has the idea of endurance. James is talking to the early Christians, encouraging them to endure despite everything going on in the world around them and despite the fact that they are being exploited by the rich.

I learned about endurance in the fifth grade. I was a huge football fan, and at that time I loved the Green Bay Packers. That year I decided to sign up for the school football team. I was just under the weight limit, which automatically made me a lineman.

At my first football drill, I was doing okay until I slipped up, and the coach made me run a lap around the quarter-mile track at the high school. I like football. I hate running. But I started running around the track anyway. I made it around one time, then I came back and got into the drill again.

About an hour later I got in trouble again because I didn't do something right, and a whole group of us had to run around the track. This time I got down to the first bend in the track and instead of running around the bend and coming back to the team, I just took off into the sunset and headed straight for the parking lot. I figured my mom would be there soon enough to pick me up. I liked football, but I didn't like playing it because I didn't have endurance.

As I got a little bit older, I realized that running was part of the game. Football is not just what we see on television. It also involves all the training beforehand that allows those players to play a good game. Endurance was something that I was not accustomed to—I didn't like it then, and there are still times when I don't like it now.

## Endurance Requires Staying on Course

How are we going to make it to the end? How are we going to endure in an evil world? What are we going to do when wickedness seems to prevail? We have to stay on course with God.

In verse 7 of this passage James uses the illustration of a farmer. The farmer knows the principles of farming. He knows the fields have to be prepared and tended and that the seeds have to be planted, watered, and fertilized—and he can't change those necessities. He knows that he has to stay on course.

As Christians, we also have to stay on course. We have to find balance in the midst of all the things going on in the world around us. It can be a very difficult task to stay balanced in this life. In our world—whether it's at the gas station or the supermarket, at work, in our churches, on the road, or whenever—we generally have an apathetic attitude toward the world, or we have a spirit of anger toward it.

Apathy is probably the easiest route. The apathetic attitude just doesn't care anymore. We are living in a wicked world, surrounded by people who don't know Jesus, so we just give up. We have our lives, our families, and our churches. We don't care that people are lost. Even though we may wake up and care about how we look, how we feel, and whether or not we are getting our rights, we don't care that people around us are lost.

When we look at the all the wicked people in the world, we

think, *If they don't want God, fine. I don't need to get all upset about it.* We slip into an attitude of total apathy.

As I travel and speak, and as I look at my own life, I think, "There are so many words, but there is so little change." Everybody talks about change, about being a devoted follower of Jesus, but where is the change? When do we realize that there are people living right next door to us who are lost? We just don't care anymore. That's the spirit of apathy.

Then there is the opposite reaction—anger. Do you ever get angry at the world? Do you ever think, *Why don't we just drop a bomb on those troublemakers, and then we'd all be better off?* It reminds me of Jonah who wanted God to simply annihilate the people of Nineveh so that he didn't have to go preach repentance to them (see Jonah 1—4).

The meanness of the world has seeped into the culture of the church so that when we look at people who don't know the Lord, we actually feel anger toward them. We see them on the roads and freeways when they cut us off and drive like maniacs. We don't think in terms of "What would Jesus do?" We think in terms of "What can I do back to them?" We think of tailgating them or slamming on our brakes if they are tailgating us. We think in terms of "I'll get you." That attitude of anger has become a part of our culture.

Philip Eaton, president of Seattle Pacific University, wrote on the theme of meanness in one of his presidential prayer letters. He said, "As a leader of a Christian organization, I feel the brunt of just this kind of meanness within the Christian community, a mean-spirited suspicion and judgment that mirrors the broader culture."[1] We have let the culture seep into our lives, and we retaliate the way the world retaliates.

As Dallas Willard wrote, "We have found ways to be Christian without being Christ-like."[2] Slowly we have come to believe that being right and getting our own way is more important than being Christlike.

The well-known slogan that young people have worn for so long, "What would Jesus do?" is a great way to make a million dollars. But do we really think that way at all? When faced with a situation in which the wicked are oppressing us, do we have the mind-set of "What would Jesus do?" Do we think about how he would respond in that situation? Or do we just want to prove that we are right to retaliate, and get revenge?

In verses 8 through 11 James speaks of patience in suffering. One thing we do know from this passage is that patience is not passivity. Patience is not just sitting around doing nothing. Patience, perseverance, and endurance are about passion and staying on course. That course is the Great Commission that Jesus gave us in Matthew 28:18–20—the mandate to go into the whole world and make disciples.

A church in Fort Lauderdale, Florida, started in 1989 with three hundred people. Over a period of about two years, they gained several new members, and they were very excited. They went away on a retreat to pat themselves on the back. There they realized that their growth had come from getting people from other churches. All they had been doing was shuffling people around, not winning any new people for Christ.

They decided to make a major turnaround. They went from three hundred members to an average attendance of twenty-three hundred on Sunday morning, not by taking people from other churches, but by leading people to Jesus. The people of that church discovered that the mission statement for their church should be to go and make disciples, and they have seen major growth because of their commitment to that mission.

## Endurance Requires Waiting on Jesus

Waiting is a difficult thing for us to do. In verse 7, James says, "Be patient, then, brothers, until the Lord's coming. See how the farmer waits." Of course, waiting does not mean doing nothing. The farmer is working, pulling weeds, watering, and doing other things while he is waiting for the growth.

Proverbs 20:22 says, "Wait for the Lord, and he will deliver you." What does it mean to wait on the Lord? It means to have a listening ear, a responsive heart, and a spiritual concentration, waiting for his leading in our lives. It doesn't mean that we just sit around and twiddle our thumbs. Martin Luther said, "Pray as if everything depends on God, then work as if everything depends on you."[3]

For example, if we are out of work, we shouldn't just sit around and say, "Lord, I need a job." We actually have to make an effort to look for one. Waiting on the Lord is an attitude that comes from having our hope and trust fully in him.

After working on crusades around the world for the last twenty years, I have realized that there is a point when I have done all I can do, and I have to leave the rest up to God. There are times in all of our lives that we have done all that we can. We just have to say, "Lord, what do you want me to do now?" and wait to hear from him.

The prophet Isaiah has some great words for us on waiting:

> Though youths grow weary and tired, and vigorous young men stumble badly, yet those who wait for the LORD will gain new strength; they will mount up with wings like eagles, they will run and not get tired, they will walk and not become weary. (Isaiah 40:30–31 NASB)

## Endurance Requires Looking for Jesus

James speaks clearly in this passage about looking for Jesus' return, what is also called his "glorious appearing" (Titus 2:13). This was a huge aspect of the Christian faith in the early church. They really expected the Lord Jesus to return any minute, and they looked forward to it. They woke up every morning eager for his return.

These early Christians lived a hard life. Their lives were not lives of luxury and ease. The prospect of going heaven and being with Jesus was far more appealing to them than continuing the lives they were living on earth. Because they were looking so diligently for Jesus to come back, that expectation affected the way they lived and the way they thought.

For most of us, the thought of Jesus' return probably doesn't enter our minds very often. It has been talked about for so long. His return has been speculated about and predicted in various fashions for years. We have invented entire theological systems to try to figure out when he is coming back. We have all heard many sermons and read numerous books warning us of his impending return, but still it doesn't seem to change the way we live our daily lives.

Do we really believe that he is coming back? Do we care that he is returning? Maybe we don't believe that Jesus really has anything to offer us in light of what we have here on earth. We have our families and a good job and a nice home and a cabin in the woods and an SUV—and life is great. There's no hurry. Sure, we want to be with Jesus some day in heaven, but for right now, we have the good life—and we want to enjoy it. Do we really *want* Jesus to return?

The reason these Christians endured—the thing that kept them going—was the belief that Jesus was going to return to take them with him to heaven. More than anything else, they desired to be with their Master, serving him and sitting at his feet.

A Russian pastor was put in prison for a long time. A letter that he wrote was smuggled out of prison, and in it he said, "With Jesus, my beloved Master, it is good everywhere. With him, I have light in the dark dungeon. I had asked him to be where I am needed, not where it is better for the outward man, but where I can bear fruit. This is my calling."[4]

Is it real? Are we looking, acting, and thinking more like Jesus every day? If we are not interested in becoming more like Jesus, and if we are not interested in becoming people who share his light with others, then our Christianity is a sham.

Are we truly devoted followers of Jesus? Is Jesus living in us? Is he living through us? May we be people who persevere patiently in the face of suffering, all the while eagerly awaiting the return of our King.

## CHAPTER 24

# THE HEART OF THE MATTER

## JAMES 5:13–20

A little girl goes to her friend's house to visit. Before dinner, the friend's mom asks the little girl if she likes broccoli with butter. The girl answers politely, "Yes, I love broccoli with butter."

As the food is being passed around the dinner table, the broccoli comes to her. The little girl just looks at it and passes it on. The mother says, "I thought you said you love broccoli with butter."

"I do," the little girl replies. "But I don't love it enough to eat it."

People have told me that they love studying the book of James. My prayer is that you and I have loved it enough to apply it to our everyday lives.

As James concludes his letter and wraps up all the things he has dealt with, he gets right to the heart of the matter: How do we live like this? How do we obey? How do we endure tough times? James says it all comes back to our relationship with God, and the time we spend in prayer. The heart of the Christian life is prayer.

Richard Foster's book *Prayer* is probably the greatest book on the subject I have ever read. In it he says, "Real prayer comes not from gritting our teeth but from falling in love."[1] Is it real? Is our experience with God so real that we are in love with him and that prayer is just an outpouring of our communication with him? In verse 16, James says, "The prayer of a righteous man is powerful and effective." He also gives us three things to pray for.

## Pray for Those Who Are Suffering

In this passage James reminds us again that endurance comes through prayer. Patience comes from God, and prayer is the way to obtain it. How do we go through a difficult time, a time when we are suffering? We don't make it on our own strength, but we make it by way of prayer, by experiencing God's strength in us.

We all know someone who is suffering. In verse 13, James says, "Is any one of you in trouble? He should pray." In the King James Version of this verse the word James uses is *afflicted*. This is deep suffering. It is not necessarily something the person brought on himself or herself, but one of those difficult situations that are a part of life.

In verse 13 James says that anyone who is suffering should pray. The word he uses for *pray* here means "to keep on praying." Every day you and I need new strength. The strength that we gain for today is not good enough for tomorrow. It takes more strength. It takes more prayer. It takes more time with God.

In my humanness, when I see a person who is suffering, my first response is "Lord, take away their suffering. Heal them physically. Give them a job. Meet their need." I want to remove their suffering. I want to remove that affliction from their life because I know it is causing pain.

But the problem—and the thing that I am always reminded of— is that affliction is the substance of growth. Even though I want to simply take affliction out of a person's life, I have to remember that God is working his plan in that individual's life to cause him or her to grow. True growth comes from adversity, affliction, and suffering.

Charles Spurgeon said, "Most of the grand truths of God have to be learned by trouble; they must be burned into us with the hot iron of affliction, otherwise we shall not truly receive them."[2]

You may be in the midst of affliction right now. You may have already gone through some suffering and are looking back and thinking, *I hope I learned my lesson already. I don't want to go through that again.* If so, then this chapter should be good news to you because your affliction and suffering are doing a great work in you and for you (see 2 Corinthians 4:16–17).

Alexander Solzhenitsyn, the great writer who spent much time in prison in the former Soviet Union, wrote: "A fact which cannot be disputed is the weakening of human personality in the West, while in the East, it has become firmer and stronger ... we have been through a spiritual training far in advance of the Western experience. The complex and deadly crush of life has produced stronger, deeper, and more interesting personalities than those generated by standardized Western well being."[3]

He wasn't slamming the West. What he was saying is that those who were in the former Soviet Union under the Communist rule lived in affliction. They were persecuted, beaten for their faith, and put in prison, and because of that suffering, they had a different Christian personality. For those of us who have never endured persecution or been jailed in the name of Christ, we do not have the same depth of personality.

As I look at my life, it seems to bounce like a Ping-Pong ball between joy and sorrow, between good days and bad days. I like the good days better than the bad days. But I am aware that the bad days produce the growth in my life.

In verse 13, James also says, "Is anyone happy? Let him sing songs of praise." In other words, whether you are having a good day or a bad day, whether you are suffering affliction now or not, the heart of the matter is prayer, whether it's the prayer of praise or the prayer of "God, give me the strength to endure this."

If you will get quiet before God, he will minister to you as no one else can. I can't get into the depths of your soul, but God is already there. Through the Holy Spirit, he will bring comfort to you as you open your heart in prayer before him.

## Pray for Those Who Are Sick

In 1988, I went to a hospital in Portland, Oregon, to prepare for my trip to Calcutta, India. The hospital staff looked in their books to see what shots I would need. Any disease or sickness you can think of, I got a shot for it. I have a little yellow card now that lists all the immunizations I have had since that time, and I have to keep it with me whenever I travel out of the country. The staff wanted to make sure I wasn't going to get sick or get anyone else sick. Illnesses and diseases are all over the world. Most often, they are just a part of life.

The Devil also has the power to make us physically and mentally sick. Then there's the issue that Paul addressed in 1 Corinthians 11:27–32 about the sicknesses that those who live in sin bring upon themselves. So we have a lot of different sicknesses, but regardless of why we are sick, James is saying we need to pray.

I don't know that God heals every person. Healing is a great mystery, but it is important enough for James to talk about here. I do believe that God can and does heal supernaturally. In verses 14 and 15 James uses two little phrases: "anoint … with oil" and "the prayer offered in faith." We know that it is God who heals. It is not the anointing or the oil or the prayer. It is the work of God that brings the healing.

There are various views on anointing with oil. Sometimes it is used in the Bible to symbolically show the belief that God is present. When the elders came and poured oil on the forehead of someone, it was a symbol of God's presence, a physical reminder that he was there. In Bible times, oil certainly had a medicinal use as well. Thus, the knowledge of medicine combined with the power of God can bring healing to a person's life.

Several years ago, I went to the doctor and found out that I had severe hearing loss in my left ear. I began to wear a hearing aid, but over the years, my hearing loss has gotten worse. Recently I went back to have more tests done, and the doctors discovered that my hearing was completely gone in that ear. As a result, I can now have an operation to restore my hearing. I am thrilled that I will be able to have my hearing back and not have to wear a hearing aid anymore. God used a combination of medicine and his gracious touch to heal me.

But there is also a healing that comes without medicine and without doctors' intervention. It doesn't happen all the time. There is a mystery to it. But when it happens, it reveals the incredible power of God.

I knew a very conservative pastor at a church in Grand Rapids,

Michigan. One day his wife was diagnosed with breast cancer, and the doctors decided that the only hope for saving her life was to remove both breasts.

The church immediately started praying. And because there happened to be an evangelistic outreach going on at the time, other pastors and churches quickly heard the news and joined in. They all decided to start praying for her. So there were members of Covenant churches and Bible churches, Baptists, Pentecostals—all kinds of people were praying for this pastor's wife.

The morning that she went in to have the surgery, as the nurses were preparing her for the operation, this woman felt that something was different in her body. She asked the nurses to check her out, so they did some more tests and X-rays, and soon discovered that the cancer had disappeared without a trace. The doctors declared it to be a miracle.

A few days later, I ran into this woman's husband, and it was interesting to see his reaction. He was happy and excited, of course, that his wife was healed, but he was also very perplexed, because some of his theology had gone right out the window, and he didn't know what to do about it. God does heal. God does go beyond what we think and what we can imagine, as Paul tells us in Ephesians 3:20.

I know what kind of people I want praying for me when I am sick. I want people praying who really believe that God can do the supernatural, and that God can go beyond what we think and imagine. I want people who say, "God, we believe you can do this thing, and in faith we are asking you to do it."

I wrote a book titled *In God We Trust ... But Only as a Last Resort*. Sometimes that is our mind-set. We will try everything else first, before we give up and go to God. James is telling us that we should pray first. This Christian life is a walk of faith, not sight (see 2 Corinthians 4:7 KJV), and therefore we need to be careful not to push God to the outside.

## Pray for Those Who Are Straying

One lady in my church has a son who has wandered away from God. She asked me one time, "Whenever you see a horse or a horse trailer, will you remember to pray for my son?" Her words really blessed me. She had picked something that would help her remember to consistently pray for her straying child.

We pray for the people who are suffering and those who are sick; we should also pray for those who have wandered from the truth. Again, we have to believe that God can do more than we could ever ask or imagine.

Often those who have strayed don't want to come back because they figure they will have to change something or do some things they don't want to do. They would rather live a self-centered life. We have to remember that only God can change hearts.

As I look at my life in relation to what James is saying, I realize that I am like so many other Christians: We all need God to help us rediscover his power, to help us rediscover the ministry of the Holy Spirit among us, and to help us rediscover our Savior, Jesus Christ, through worship, through the experiences of life, and through the study of his Word. Because when it comes down to it, we all want to be able to say, "Yes, this life with God is real."

That is what James is getting at. He is asking each one of us: "Are you just walking through the motions, or is this something that is real, something that goes beyond the Sunday morning experience? Have you truly experienced God? If you have experienced him, are you touching other people with his love?"

Is it real? That is a great question, one that I can't answer for you, just as you can't answer it for me. Is it real for you?

# READERS' GUIDE

*FOR PERSONAL REFLECTION*
*OR GROUP DISCUSSION*

# READERS' GUIDE

## Chapter 1

1. "A carefree, trial-less existence is nothing less than impossible." If this is true, why do so many people, including Christians, try so hard to avoid pain and suffering?

2. "[James] wanted to remind them that though trials were inevitable, they could choose how they were going to respond to those difficult times." Read Jesus' words in Matthew 5:12. What are our reasons for choosing to respond with joy in suffering?

3. "During a trial, choose joy—don't contaminate that mind-set by mixing it with fear or worry or unrest." How can you choose to be joyful in a trial you are experiencing right now?

4. "James says to count our trials as pure joy because God is at work in our lives doing something amazing." When have you seen God use a difficult situation to do the impossible in your life? How can you keep that perspective during a trial?

5. "But if we focus on the eternal, we can consider the end result God has planned for us and rejoice." Read 1 Peter 1:6–8. How can you stay aware of the "big picture" God has for you?

6. "Will we view our trials as the means God uses to draw us closer to him and say, 'Yes, Lord, I accept the trial. I want to learn whatever you want to teach me through this situation'?" Have you asked the Lord to teach you what he wants you to learn through your current trials? If not, will you do so right now?

## Chapter 2

1. "What God desires from us is that emptiness that genuinely seeks out his wisdom." Are you experiencing emptiness? If so, are you genuinely seeking out God's wisdom for your life today?

2. Read Matthew 7:7–11. Do you really believe that God will give you his wisdom if you ask for it? What underlying belief(s) keeps you from praying for the fullness of God's wisdom right now?

3. "The Bible commands us to pursue wisdom, to seek it out." How should this fact change your prayers during trials?

4. "Asking for wisdom is a habit that is formed by constant use." Who or what will enable you to form this habit of asking for wisdom?

5. "In this passage James is saying that without faith, we cannot expect to gain wisdom." What does James 1:3–4 say is the result (or purpose) of trials? What does our faith have to do with God's wisdom?

6. "In order for God to give us wisdom, we must act in faith, and we must value our relationship with him as more important than anything else in this world." How do your priorities line up with this statement? What daily changes can you begin to make to place your relationship with God as your first priority?

7. "[God] knows whether your heart is divided or whether it is completely his." Is your heart divided, or is it completely God's? Do you believe he is capable of turning an unstable, divided heart into a heart that is sold out for him?

## Chapter 3

1. "I listened to this man speak joyfully about his life. Although he had lost so much … he had joy because he knew he was a child of the King." If you lost everything you own, would joy still characterize your life? Why or why not?

2. "We can rejoice in trials, even ones that cause us to lose worldly riches, because God knows us, and loves us, and he will not forsake us." Do you believe that God takes care of every aspect of our lives, even our monetary needs?

3.  "'You cannot serve both God and Money' (Matthew 6:24)." Take a look at your checkbook, at your day-to-day worries, at the way you approach your job. Based on these things, whom or what do you honestly serve?

4.  "You do not have to be a victim of the American dream. You do not have to listen to what the world tells you about what to have and what to own in order to be successful." What are the differences between an "American dream" life and a life of service to God? How do those differences influence your financial goals?

5.  "One day all of us, the rich and the poor, are going to stand before the throne, and God will not only look at what we have done but also at how we have used our resources." If you stood before the throne of God today or tonight, would he be pleased with the way you are using the resources he gave you?

6.  "We are living in this world, but what happens here will affect the next world." In what ways can you remind yourself of the eternal significance of today's decisions, especially in the area of finances?

## Chapter 4

1.  "We are always looking for somebody to blame, and that statement is never truer than when it comes to our sins and failures." Do you tend to blame other people for sins in your own life?

2.  "We have missed the mark of God's perfection. That's what makes the message of the cross such a glorious thing." What is it about the cross that offers us hope in the face of our personal sins?

3.  "We have created in our own minds what a bad sin is and what an okay sin is. Are there sins that God hates more than others?" Do you find yourself "classifying" sin, with your weaknesses labeled as "okay" sin? If so, are you willing to ask God to transform your view of sin to be like his?

4.  "Jesus said that these things that are inside of us are who we really are. Sometimes I look in the mirror, and I may like what I see on the outside, but I don't like what I know is inside. It can be a very frightening thing to face one's own sin." Do you like what is inside you? If not, are you willing to change it?

5. "[God's] holiness encompasses moral purity, ethical beauty, and moral perfection." How does a morally perfect God view our "little" sins (white lies, gossip, breaking traffic laws, etc.)?

6. "The sins in our lives sometimes make us want to run and hide from God. We look at our lives and see our shortcomings, and we are afraid." What is it about God that allows us to approach him with whatever sin we are committing?

## Chapter 5

1. "Whether it is to think something wrong, to say something wrong, or to do something wrong, we are all tempted." What are your biggest areas of temptation? How will identifying your weaknesses help you to protect yourself against willfully entering tempting situations?

2. "[Joni Eareckson Tada] said that God doesn't give our morality a vacation. It is not okay to peacefully coexist with temptation in our lives." Are you peacefully coexisting with temptation in your life? Or do you deal with it promptly?

3. "People were under a lot of stress, so they turned to crime as a release from their situations.... As believers, we have to be especially careful of stressful times, because during these stressful times temptation can bombard us even more than usual." What safeguards do you have set up (or will you now set up) to protect yourself from sinning in times of stress?

4. "Sin happens when we yield our wills to the temptation. That's when we get in trouble. The sin usually starts small, but when it grows big, it can destroy our lives." Do you know any people who have allowed temptation to lead them into sin and eventually into "death" (of a career, a marriage, a ministry, etc.)? What small sins in your life need to be dealt with so that this is not true of you?

5. "We need to balance our lives so that we have time for God, because without that relationship, we have no resistance to temptation." How can you make sure your life is in balance so you will have God's strength to resist temptation?

6. "I have had too many friends whose lives have been destroyed because they thought it was going to be okay to sin.... Yes, God

understands our weaknesses, but he gives us the power to overcome them." Have you asked God to give you his power to resist temptation in your weak areas? If not, are you willing to do so now?

## Chapter 6

1. "Don't be deceived into thinking that somehow God is trying to trip you up and destroy you. He cares for you even more than an earthly father cares for his children." Do you know a father who genuinely, enthusiastically cares for his children? How does God's care outshine even the strongest fatherly love?

2. "God does not give us temptations. He gives us good and perfect gifts, and we receive those gifts every day." What are those gifts that God has specifically given to you? Make a list (as long as you can!) of all the little and big gifts God has given you.

3. "God our Father is waiting with open arms for us. He is running toward us, and he wants us to run to him." In what ways have you felt God's "open arms" and his "running toward" you in the past few months?

4. "God's character does not change. He doesn't have any shadows. He doesn't change like the seasons.... In a world of uncertainties, we can have confidence in who God is." Read Matthew 7:24–27. Is your life built upon the rock of God's unchanging character and trustworthiness? How do you know?

5. "God has given us a spiritual birth that has made us different people." How are your life, your heart, and your mind different from what they were before your spiritual birth?

## Chapter 7

1. "For some people, listening is a real gift. You may be very good at listening. Others, like me, have to work hard at learning to listen." If listening isn't your natural gift, how can you begin to listen more than you speak?

2. "François Fenelon wrote, 'God never ceases to speak to us, but the noise of the world without and the tumult of our passions within bewilder us and prevent us from listening to him.'" Can

you hear God's voice speaking to you? If not, what may be the cause of the "silence" (remembering that God never stops communicating with us)?

3. "First, we study the Bible." Do you actively study God's Word? If not, how can you make Bible study a part of your daily schedule?

4. "Meditation means filling our minds with the Word of God, and then pondering it, reflecting on it, and considering how it might pertain to us." Choose a passage of Scripture to meditate on this week, asking God to make it real to your life.

5. "Do you have times when you think the Lord may be speaking to you to do something, but you aren't sure? I encourage you to do it anyway. See what happens. You may be very surprised. Be open to God's prompting." Do you think God is prompting you to do something right now? If so, are you willing to follow through with obedience?

6. "The wonderful part is that you can meditate and contemplate while changing diapers, mowing the lawn, or sitting in traffic. Meditation is a matter of the heart." How can you prepare your heart to meditate in the midst of daily activities?

## Chapter 8

1. "The word *do* indicates a continuous action. Doing what Jesus commanded should be a part of our lifestyles." Do you obey Jesus' commands on a continual basis? Is obedience a part of your lifestyle? Why or why not?

2. "James is telling these Christians, 'Don't just study the Word. Don't just look at it. Learn it, know it, understand it, and pass that information along to someone else…. The reason you study and meditate on God's Word is to live it.'" How does your personal Bible study affect other people's lives? Can others tell that you study God's Word?

3. Read Matthew 6:1–4. How does Jesus instruct us to do good works? Whom do our rewards come from, men or God?

4. "True followers of Jesus obey *all* his commands." Are you obeying Jesus Christ's teachings? Or, are you fooling yourself by merely listening to the Word?

5. "True joy comes when we say, 'Lord, I want to be a doer of your Word. I want to be obedient to what you've told me to do.'" Do you have the true joy that comes from a life of obedience?

## Chapter 9

1. "James is concerned because ceremony has become so important to the church that it is overlooking the basics." Is this ambivalence true of your spiritual walk? If so, how can you return to the basics of loving and serving?

2. "What comes out of our mouths, the words we say when we think no one is looking, reveal our true colors. Words are like a window to the soul." What is seen through the window of your soul?

3. "We would probably never put the sins of speech in a category with immorality or any of the other grave sins, but James is very clear here. If we say we are Christians, and our words do not prove it, our religion is a waste of time." How do you view an uncontrolled tongue? How does God view it? Does your tongue prove or disprove your religion?

4. "We can certainly enjoy life. Separation from the world has to do with our attitudes, what's in our heart, and what's important to us." How can we live in the world but not be part of it?

5. "God has something for each of us to do. Have we discovered it? Are we doing it? Are we being the people God wants us to become?" Do you know what God wants you to do? If not, will you ask him to show you while you continue to obey him? If so, are you wholeheartedly pursuing that purpose?

6. "James wants us to be careful about the world, because our primary mission here is to be dispensers of God's love to people. We are supposed to shine forth, to be light, and to lift up God to others." How does your life shine forth light in the world? How do you want it to shine forth?

## Chapter 10

1. "Even though we may love people for who they are, it is often easier to love those with a lot of money or possessions." Why do you think

this is true? What intentional changes can you implement to love people for who they are, regardless of their status or money?

2. "It is easy for us to say that we are Christians when nothing bad is happening to us." Why does God allow Christians to go through hard times?

3. "They have no ties to the present world. Thus, in many ways, it is much easier to be tied to the next world." How can you release some of your ties to this world in order to be tied to the next world?

4. "James reminds them that their importance does not come from being with important people." Where do you find your personal value, from people or from God?

5. "People come to church expecting to find a place to belong, a place to worship and serve, but instead what they often find is a house of special interest groups and church politics." What can you do in your church to make it a place where people can belong, worship, and serve?

6. "James says that if we show favoritism—whether it is within the church or outside of it—then we are sinning." Has God revealed to you that this is an area of your life that needs to be changed? If so, how can you stop sinning in this way?

7. "Power offers an easy substitute for the hard task of love. It is easier to be God than to love God; it is easier to control people than to love people." What holds you back from letting God be God in other people's lives? What will you do to overcome that obstacle?

## Chapter 11

1. "Showing mercy is a display of love, and should happen on a regular basis. It should be a way of life." Does the mercy you show prove the reality of God in your life?

2. "However, it is still an intense thought to consider that we will one day stand before God and give an account of our lives. It is certainly a cause for reflection and self-examination." Are you prepared for judgment day? What will God say about your life and faith?

3. "We live carelessly in many ways because we are not acutely aware of our impending judgment." How would a proper understanding of the coming judgment change the way you make choices and live your life?

4. "But Jesus requires mercy. Mercy is an aspect of God's love." To whom do you need to extend mercy today? Are you delaying in obeying Jesus' commandment to do so? If so, is that action revealing the love of God?

5. "If we say that we are followers of Jesus, then we should be treating people in the same way, showing mercy to them even when they don't deserve it. One of the greatest ways that we can show mercy is through forgiveness." Read Matthew 18:21–35. Do you behave like the unmerciful servant, or is your heart constantly reflecting on your cancelled debt?

## Chapter 12

1. "James says that works done out of love are evidence of faith, for faith is active." How is your faith active?

2. "As that individual walks with Christ, his life will display the fruit of the Spirit through his works." Do the works in your life prove that you have true faith?

3. "We must be prepared to choose Christianity and commit ourselves to the consequences of the choice. This means believing not just with our emotions, but also with our wills." How is Christianity a choice of your will? How does that choice impact your day-to-day living?

4. "We don't want someone telling us what to do. Very few of us can honestly say, 'I surrender all.'" Is there an area of your life that you have been holding on to? If so, are you willing to ask God to soften your heart so you can truly "surrender all"?

5. "Saving faith activates the intellect, the emotions, and the will. That kind of faith says, 'Yes, I will follow Jesus.'" How does your will back up the decision of your intellect and emotions to follow Jesus?

6. "James tells us that faith without works, faith without change, faith without mercy, is not real faith at all. It's bogus faith." How do the

people around you know that your faith is real? What changes has faith made in your life?

7.  Read Matthew 25:34–40. For whom does Jesus say our good works are done? How can you practically implement good works in your life?

## Chapter 13

1.  "Every morning that we wake up we need faith, so that we can abide with Jesus in every situation we encounter." What situations in your life this week require Jesus' continuing help in your unbelief?

2.  "If we are truly followers of Jesus, when we see a brother or sister in need, we have to do something about that need." What people in your life need you to care for their needs? What will you do today to care for those needs?

3.  "Abraham's faith was judged by his actions. When God asked him to do what seemed unthinkable, he did it." What unthinkable thing has God asked you to do? Caring for needy people? Giving up prejudices? Rejoicing in trials? How does your faith measure up when judged by your response to that "unthinkable" instruction?

4.  "Sadly, though, we can live year after year without having a new thought about God and about his greatness and majesty." What fuels you to have great thoughts about God? What makes your thoughts of God smaller and less meaningful?

5.  "God blows away the boxes we may try to put him in. He is bigger than our finite minds; he goes far beyond what we can think or imagine." Does God fit neatly inside your "God box," or do you allow him to daily blow away your perceptions of who he is and what he does? In what ways can you begin to authentically see God's greatness and power?

6.  Read Psalms 135, 136, 138, and 139. What do these passages teach us about God's character and his involvement in human lives?

## Chapter 14

1.  "Our faith is important in activating our will, in motivating and inspiring us to do something for God." What are you motivated and inspired to do for God? What part does faith play in your actions?

2. "Emotions are generated by thoughts. Abraham ... allowed his thoughts to dwell on God's awesomeness and power, and he was able to step out in faith." Where do your thoughts dwell? On God's attributes, or on yourself?

3. "I certainly have times when I get very low.... But every time that happens, I can trace it back to my thinking. I have had shallow or weak thoughts about God." What or who ignites great thoughts about God in your life? What intentional ways can you build your schedule around things that bring your mind back to God?

4. "Living faith is that faith that causes us to step out, that faith that causes us to activate our wills in obedience to God." How does your faith prove to be "alive"?

5. "As long as we try to control God, our faith is stagnant. It is when he takes us into the deep waters that our faith grows." Think about a difficult situation you have recently faced. How did your faith grow and mature through that experience?

6. "We stop dreaming because we don't believe God can really do what we envision. We think that the God of the Bible is gone, that he doesn't do miracles anymore." What dreams would you have for your life if you believed that God really could do anything? What holds you back from believing in his miraculous power?

7. "If we can't point to a time or a situation in which we saw God do something for us, our faith is not growing. We need to get into situations in which the only way out is by God's help." What bold steps of faith is God calling you to take right now? Have you asked him to help you as you obey him?

## Chapter 15

1. "Whether we are in the classroom, at work, at home, or just dealing with people on a daily basis, we are all teaching." Whom do you "teach" on a regular basis?

2. "We are not going to become better Christians by getting more knowledge." How can you act upon the knowledge you already have?

3. "No matter how old or how knowledgeable we get, we can always continue to learn and grow." Is your faith continually growing? If not, what is inhibiting that growth?

4. "In 1 John 2:5–6 the writer says of Jesus, 'This is how we know we are in him: Whoever claims to live in him must walk as Jesus did.'" In what areas do you walk as Jesus did? In what areas do you need to change and mature?

5. "Too many of us have stopped trying to learn. We are stuck, just like those pottery students, trying to make the perfect life." What is the "perfect life" according to God's standards? How does that differ from the life you are striving for?

6. Read Matthew 5:19. What did Jesus say about those who break his commandments and teach others to do the same? What does he say about those who practice and teach his commandments?

## Chapter 16

1. "They have the power to encourage, and the power to discourage, the power to liberate, and the power to manipulate. Although they can't be physically seen or felt, their power is immense." Can you recall any times this week that words spoken by you or to you have made an impact on your life? If so, describe them.

2. "The tongue does not act alone. Our words come from a deeper source—our hearts." What do your words (and tone of voice) reveal about the condition of your heart?

3. "If we bring forth words of life, and if our words bring healing and encouragement to people, those words will come back to us as well." Can you recall a time when you needed a word of encouragement, hope, or healing? Did you get it? When can you give "words of life" to others?

4. "What we say during our lives is often what we will be remembered for after we die." If you were to die today, what would your words say about the person you were and the life you lived?

5. "Words are potent and powerful. They can inspire hope, or they can destroy dreams. They can start a war, or they can heal a heart." Do

you think about the power of your words before you speak them? Should you? If so, why?

6. "We give direction with our words. I look at my life and wonder, *How am I at directing other people?*" Do people wilt or prosper under the direction of your words? How so?

## *Chapter 17*

1. Read Matthew 7:16–20. What do your words ("fruit") communicate about who you are as a person?

2. Read Proverbs 26:20. What is the best way to end the quarrels and dissension around you?

3. "From talk radio shows to television commercials to political debates, our speech is frequently negative and criticizing." As Christians, how should our speech be different? Why should it be different?

4. "And every time it is retold, the gossip is mutated until it barely resembles the original comment." How can you stop gossip from getting out of hand in your own life?

5. "Unfortunately, gossip is usually done with the intent to harm someone else. Shared information about someone else's life almost always seems to be negative." Read Matthew 22:37–40. How can we practice the second great commandment when tempted to or confronted by gossip?

6. "It may have started ten or twenty years ago, but the new pastor can still smell the lingering effects of that fire. He can see the lasting consequences of gossip and slander." How have gossip and slander affected your life? Why is it so important to limit the things you say about other people?

7. "On the other hand, we have all known people who have encouraged us at one time or another. A word of affirmation or affection can be just as powerful as a word of gossip or slander." In what specific ways can you use your tongue for good and not for evil today?

## Chapter 18

1. "It [wisdom] is taking knowledge, the things that we know, and applying it to our lives to make them better, to bring them more in line with what the Lord wants us to be, and how he wants us to act." According to this definition, how wise are you?

2. "Worldly wisdom comes from pure selfishness. It is concerned with attaining, with pushing forward in life." Does worldly wisdom cause you to envy other people's possessions, positions, or personalities? If so, what should you do about it?

3. Read Luke 9:23–25. How does Jesus' wisdom compare with worldly wisdom? Which one characterizes your life?

4. "There is a cost to following Jesus. He did not teach us just so we would have a theoretical, abstract idea to follow." In what practical ways do you need to follow Jesus rather than merely "believing in Jesus" theoretically or abstractly?

5. "You may be in a situation in life in which worldly wisdom has influenced you to buy into a lie, and now you need some of God's wisdom." Are you facing a situation like this? If so, have you asked God to give you his wisdom?

6. "God didn't save and redeem us so that we could live on earth to accumulate stuff and say, 'Isn't life great?'" What is the purpose of your life? If you don't know, have you asked God for the wisdom promised in James 1:5?

## Chapter 19

1. "This passage in James means so much to me personally, because I find myself in great need of God's wisdom." In what area(s) of your life do you need God's wisdom in a specific way?

2. "The motivation for what we do and the decisions we make should be pure." What motivates you to serve the Lord? Are those motivations pure?

3. "A considerate person is not mean-spirited or withdrawn. It is a person who wants to reach out with gentleness to those who do not know Jesus." How do you treat unbelievers?

4. "To be submissive is to be compliant and willing to change, willing to say, 'I was wrong in that situation, I'm sorry.'" Can other people approach you, or do you have a chip on your shoulder?

5. "Some believers have an appearance of goodness in their actions and in the way they treat others, but they lack the sincerity and authenticity that should distinguish true followers of Christ." How does your "Christian appearance" compare to who you honestly are? What keeps you from being authentic with the body of Christ?

6. "Only [God] can help us give up those areas in our lives where we have been using worldly wisdom, and not his wisdom." What are those areas in your life? Have you asked God to replace worldly wisdom with his wisdom?

7. Read Matthew 5:3–12. What kind of people did Jesus call blessed? Does that list describe your life?

## Chapter 20

1. "Instead of studying the Word of God and being edified, they were all trying to assert themselves by fighting over what positions they occupied." Is this true of your life?

2. "Instead of being known for the love they had for one another ... they were known for fighting, hatred, and discord." What are you known for in your interactions with other Christians?

3. "The phrase 'friendship with the world' means to be approved by the world." Are you friends with the world or with God? How does your life prove it?

4. "The enemy has one goal, and that is to separate us from God. He can't take away our salvation, but he wants us to have no prayer life, no intimacy, no walk with God, no power, and no interest in spiritual things." Do you believe that the Devil exists as a liar and deceiver, trying to separate people from God? Are you aware of his presence and his evil schemes?

5. "For many of us, all we know of God is what we have read. We have read of his power, his omnipotence, and what he has done in the past, but we haven't observed him or experienced him personally."

How do you observe and experience God personally rather than merely possessing knowledge about him?

6. "God made it very clear that if we truly and earnestly seek him, we will surely find him.... We have to have a passion to pursue God, to see him do miraculous things." How passionate is your pursuit of God? What drives you to seek him?

## Chapter 21

1. "Here James talks to those who are arrogant and wealthy, those who are making plans and calculating their lives without God." How do you include (or not include) God in your life plans and preparations?

2. "Even in our complex life, when we have to think about so many things, we are fools if we forget about what's going to happen at the end." How does the thought of eternity change your life in the present time?

3. "Here James is calling us to seriously understand that our lives are in the hands of God. No matter what plans we make, God numbers our days. He knows the ending; we don't." Do you consider your days as "numbered"? How would this proper perspective change your lifestyle or goals?

4. "One thing I understand—when I die, I die alone. I will stand there before the Lord by myself." How prepared are you for the day when you stand alone before God Almighty?

5. "Eventually, our lives will end, and then what will matter is whether or not we knew Jesus as Savior." Do you know Jesus as your personal Savior? If not, have you considered whether you are prepared for eternity?

6. "But for those of us who have trusted in Christ as Savior, we do not need to fear death. We have a blessed hope that when our time on earth is up, we have a perfect heavenly home." As a Christian, do you fear death? If so, ask God to give you an eternal perspective of your life.

## Chapter 22

1. "Money tells us about what we value, what we hold dear, what is important in our lives. Money talks about our hearts." What does your money say about what you value, about what is important in your life, about the condition of your heart?

2. "But God doesn't like it when we rely on our savings as the means to bail us out of trouble, when we put our trust in our savings instead of in him." Where does your security come from? Would you trust God more or less if you lost your money?

3. "Another word for hoarding is *greed*. Sometimes we know there is greed in our lives, but at other times we don't even recognize it." Is there greed in your life? How can you change greed to generosity?

4. "How we use the money God has given us speaks volumes about our priorities. Money also tells us whether we are honest or dishonest with what we have been given." How does your character stand up when your money habits and practices are examined?

5. "We can be dishonest simply by not giving back to God what really belongs to him. God has not just suggested that we give to him—he has absolutely commanded it." Do you obey this command no matter what your financial situation is?

## Chapter 23

1. "We are living in a wicked world, surrounded by people who don't know Jesus, so we just give up." Are you apathetic toward the lost people in your life?

2. "We don't think in terms of 'What would Jesus do?' We think in terms of 'What can I do back to them?'" Is this true of your life in your interactions with other people?

3. "Patience is not just sitting around doing nothing. Patience, perseverance, and endurance are about passion and staying on course." Is your patience also marked with an obedience that keeps you on course?

4. "What does it mean to wait on the Lord? It means to have a listening ear, a responsive heart, and a spiritual concentration, waiting for his leading in our lives." In what way are you waiting on the Lord right

now? Are you listening, being responsive, and concentrating on his leading?

5. "Because they were looking so diligently for Jesus to come back, that expectation affected the way they lived and the way they thought." How often do you think about Jesus' return? How would your life be different if it was always on your mind?

6. "If we are not interested in becoming more like Jesus, and if we are not interested in becoming people who share his light with others, then our Christianity is a sham." Is your Christian faith authentic or a sham? How so?

## Chapter 24

1. "How do we live like this? How do we obey? How do we endure tough times? James says it all comes back to our relationship with God, and the time we spend in prayer. The heart of the Christian life is prayer." How do you live an authentic Christian life? Is it through prayer?

2. "James reminds us again that endurance comes through prayer. Patience comes from God, and prayer is the way to obtain it." Think of a trial or rough time you are experiencing right now. Have you prayed for patience and endurance in it?

3. "Affliction is the substance of growth.... True growth comes from adversity, affliction, and suffering." How does this truth change the way you pray for other people who are experiencing hard times?

4. "I want people praying who really believe that God can do the supernatural, and that God can go beyond what we think and imagine." Do you believe that God has the power to supernaturally heal people? Do you come to him with this faith when someone you know is sick?

5. "We will try everything else first before we give up and go to God. James is telling us that we should pray first." Do you find yourself trying everything else before going to God? How can you change in order to put God first in your life?

6. "She had picked something that would help her remember to consistently pray for her straying child." Do you know someone who really needs your prayers? Think of an object or event (such as a yield sign,

someone's house, or a particular smell) that can remind you to pray for that person consistently.

7. "We have to remember that only God can change hearts." Ask God to first change your heart, to give you a passion for the lost, sick, and hurting. Then, ask God to change their hearts so that they will place him on the throne of their lives.

# NOTES

## Introduction
1. Charles Templeton, *Farewell to God* (Toronto: McClelland and Stewart Ltd., 1999).
2. 2004 poll by the Gallup Organization, based on 12,043 interviews. Maximum margin of sampling error ±3 percentage points, published online at: www.gallup.com/poll/content/default.aspx?ci=14410. Copyright © 2005—The Gallup Organization.

## Chapter 1
1. Albert Ellery Bergh, ed., *The Writings of Thomas Jefferson: The Memorial Edition*, 19 volumes, http://www.constitution.org/tj/jeff.htm.
2. James Strong, *Strong's Exhaustive Concordance of the Bible* (Nashville: Abingdon, 1890), "Greek Dictionary of the New Testament," s.v., "testing," entry #1383 *dokimion*, 24.
3. William Barclay, *The Letters of James and Peter* (Louisville: Westminster John Knox Press, 1960), 51.
4. Oswald Chambers, "October 25: Submitting to God's Purpose," in *My Utmost for His Highest* (New York: Dodd, Mead, & Company, 1935), 299.

## Chapter 2
1. Helen Keller, "Three Days to See," *The Atlantic Monthly*, 151 (January 1933): 35–42.

## Chapter 3
1. Carroll E. Simcox, *3,000 Quotations on Christian Themes* (Grand Rapids, MI: Baker Book House, 1988), 96.

## Chapter 4
1. C. S. Lewis, *Mere Christianity* (New York: Harper Collins, 2001), 192.
2. Nancy Gibbs, "The Secret of Life," *Time*, February 17, 2003.
3. Westminster Confession of Faith, "Chapter 11," Public Domain. Quoted in http://www.reformed.org/documents/wcf_with_proofs.

## Chapter 5
1. Mark Water, *The New Encyclopedia of Christian Quotations* (Grand Rapids, MI: Baker Books, 2000), 925.
2. Joni Eareckson Tada, *Secret Strength: For Those Who Search* (Portland,

OR: Multnomah Press, 1988), 30.
3. Dietrich Bonhoeffer, *Creation and Fall/Temptation: Two Biblical Studies* (New York: Touchstone, 1983), 132.

## Chapter 6
1. Henri Nouwen, *The Return of the Prodigal Son* (New York: Image/Doubleday, 1994), 95–96.
2. Richard Hammer, "Our Wonderous Heavens," in *The Christian Reader*, December 1985.
3. James S. Hewett, *Illustrations Unlimited* (Wheaton, IL: Tyndale House Publishers, 1988), 93.

## Chapter 7
1. Mark Water, *The New Encyclopedia of Christian Quotations* (Grand Rapids, MI: Baker Books, 2000), 614.
2. *Merriam-Webster's Collegiate Dictionary*, 10th ed., s.v. "contemplate" and "contemplation."
3. Joyce Huggett, *The Joy of Listening: Hearing the Many Ways God Speaks to Us* (Downers Grove, IL: InterVarsity Press, 1986).
4. Mark Water, *The New Encyclopedia of Christian Quotations* (Grand Rapids, MI: Baker Books, 2000), 50.
5. Ibid., 49.

## Chapter 8
1. Mark Water, *The New Encyclopedia of Christian Quotations* (Grand Rapids, MI: Baker Books, 2000), 694.
2. Rick Manoff, citation paraphrased from "The U.F.O. Controversy," *Rays from the Rose Cross*, March/April 1996, 51.

## Chapter 9
1. David McLellan, *Karl Marx: Selected Writings* (Oxford: Oxford University Press, 2000), 71.
2. Mark Water, *The New Encyclopedia of Christian Quotations* (Grand Rapids, MI: Baker Books, 2000), 858.
3. Wayne Curtis, "The Methuselah Report: Living to be 120 might be attainable, but is it desirable?" *AARP Bulletin*, July/August 2004, http://www.aarp.org/bulletin/yourhealth/a2004-07-07-methuselah.html.
4. From the International Albert Schweitzer Association, published online at: www.schweitzer.org/english/ase/asebio.htm.

## Chapter 11
1. Jonathan Edwards, "Sinners in the Hands of an Angry God" in *The Norton Anthology of American Literature*, vol. 1, (New York: W. W. Norton & Company, Inc., 1979), 253.
2. Frank Mead, *The Encyclopedia of Religious Quotations* (London: Peter Davies, 1965), 301.
3. James S. Hewett, *Illustrations Unlimited* (Wheaton, IL: Tyndale House Publishers, 1988), 345.

4. Dottie Enrico, "'Girl' tells whole story of child in that photo," *USA TODAY*, August 10, 2000, 6D.

## Chapter 12
1. Martin Luther, "Justification by Faith," Public Domain. Quoted in www.thecaveonline.com/4PEH/reformdocument.html.
2. Judson W. Van DeVenter, "I Surrender All," *Baptist Hymnal* (Nashville: Convention Press, 1975).
3. Andrew Murray, "Ye Are the Branches" from Absolute Surrender and Other Addresses. (Chicago: Moody Press, 1895). (Public Domain.)

## Chapter 13
1. Mahatma Gandhi. Quoted in http://www.thinkexist.com/English/Author/x/Author_3569_6.htm.

## Chapter 14
1. *Atlantic Journal*, (June 16, 1833), Public Domain. Quoted in http://churchlivingspirit.org/Sermons/HowToLiveAlessAnxiousLife.html.

## Chapter 15
1. John Frye, *Jesus, the Pastor* (Grand Rapids, MI: Zondervan, 2000), 116.

## Chapter 16
1. Blaise Pascal. Quoted in http://www.nobilitypress.com/quotes/quotes_W.html.
2. *The Voice of the Martyrs: Extreme Devotion* (Nashville: W Publishing Group, 2001), 74.
3. Arthur Lenehan, *The Best of Bits & Pieces* (Fairfield, NJ: Economics Press, 1994).

## Chapter 17
1. Corinne J. Naden. *The Chicago Fire* (New York: Franklin Watts, Inc., 1969), 2, 22, 50.
2. *Merriam-Webster's Collegiate Dictionary*, 10th ed., s.v. "slander."

## Chapter 18
1. Mark Water. *The New Encyclopedia of Christian Quotations* (Grand Rapids, MI: Baker Books, 2000), 1119.
2. Thomas Watson, Quoted in http://www.globalprovince.com/computers.htm.
3. Ken Olson, Quoted in http://www.globalprovince.com/computers.htm.
4. Mark Water. *The New Encyclopedia of Christian Quotations* (Grand Rapids, MI: Baker Books, 2000), 932.
5. Bette Midler, Quoted in http://www.brainyquote.com/quotes/quotes/b/bettemidle136173.html.

## Chapter 20

1. *Today in the Word* (Moody Bible Institute: June 1988). Originally published in *Personnel Journal.*
2. Charles Baudelaire. Quoted in http://www.quotationspage.com/quote/30777.html.
3. Mark Water. *The New Encyclopedia of Christian Quotations* (Grand Rapids, MI: Baker Books, 2000), 1135.
4. Lee Strobel, *The Case for Faith* (Grand Rapids, MI: Zondervan, 2000), 255.

## Chapter 21

1. Lou Erickson. Quoted in http://www.borntomotivate.com/LouErickson.html.
2. Dr. Maurice Rawlings, *Beyond Death's Door* (New York: Bantam Books, 1978, reprint 1991).
3. James S. Hewett. *Illustrations Unlimited* (Wheaton, IL: Tyndale House Publishers, 1988), 151.

## Chapter 23

1. Philip Eaton. Presidential Prayer Letter, August 2000.
2. Dallas Willard. *Renovation of the Heart: Putting on the Character of Christ* (Colorado Springs: NavPress Publishing Group, 2002), 239.
3. Martin Luther. Quoted in http://www.sermonillustrations.com/a-z/p/prayer.htm.
4. *The Voice of the Martyrs: Extreme Devotion* (Nashville: W Publishing Group, 2001), 315.

## Chapter 24

1. Mark Water. *The New Encyclopedia of Christian Quotations* (Grand Rapids, MI: Baker Books, 2000), 761.
2. Rev. Charles H. Spurgeon. "Salvation of the Lord." Delivered on Sabbath Morning, May 10, 1857 at the Music Hall, Royal Surrey Gardens, Public Domain. Quoted in http://www.spurgeon.org/sermons/0131.htm.
3. Alexander Solzhenitsyn, "A World Split Apart," *National Review Online,* June 6, 2003, http://www.nationalreview.com/document/document060603.asp.

# ABOUT THE AUTHOR AND ETERNITY MINDED MINISTRIES

Over the past twenty years across America and in thirty-seven countries, Daniel Owens has proclaimed the gospel of Jesus Christ and has communicated the need for personal renewal to hundreds of thousands of people.

*Christianity Today* profiled Dan Owens as one of fifty "Up and Comers"—one of "the many faithful disciples God has raised up to lead the church into the new millennium." This recognition came because of his unique ability to adapt his contemporary messages to impact any audience. The British publication *Evangelism Today* says, "Dan Owens has a winsome way with words, and a smile that makes it possible to say almost anything without giving offense."

Dan Owens is also the author of *Sharing Christ When You Feel You Can't* and *In God We Trust ... But Only as a Last Resort.* He has helped train thousands of Christians to build bridges to the unchurched world. Dan is an engaging speaker who is passionate about communicating the need for personal renewal.

Before he founded Eternity Minded Ministries, Dan Owens served with the Luis Palau Evangelistic Association as director of training and as an associate evangelist for eleven years.

Dan Owens is a graduate of Christian Heritage College (San Diego, California) and Multnomah Seminary (Portland, Oregon). An approved Staley lecturer for colleges and universities, Dan has been a featured speaker at Alive, Creation Festival, Spirit Fest Midwest, and other youth events across the country and around the world.

Whether speaking to thousands of teenagers at a rally, college students at a university, adults at a mission conference, or families at a festival, Dan Owens is at home in front of people. Listening to this fun, dynamic, and compelling speaker, audiences are moved to consider eternity!

Before crusade and festival meetings, Dan Owens and his associates train Christians in friendship evangelism, counseling, and follow-up. This training increases the effectiveness of the evangelistic outreach and equips church members for ongoing evangelism long after the crusade or festival ends.

Now living in the San Francisco Bay area, Dan and his wife, Deb, have been married for more than twenty-five years. They have three sons: Ben (born in 1982), Jordan (born in 1985), and Taylor (born in 1996).

For more information contact:

Eternity Minded Ministries
P. O. Box 502101
San Diego, CA 92150
(760) 480-8752
info@eternityminded.org

### Free Online Resources

Be sure to log onto *www.danowens.org* today to write a brief letter to Daniel Owens. He would love to hear how this book has helped you enjoy a more authentic faith!

On the *www.danowens.org* Web site, you will discover a treasure chest of free ministry resources and Eternity Minded Ministries updates. You can also sign up for Dan Owens's free ministry newsletter so you can keep in touch with him, pray for his ministry, and invite him to speak at your church or conference.

Online you can learn when Dan Owens will be speaking in your area and listen to some of his most popular messages and radio programs. You can also request a free CD.

Check it out today!

Ask for additional copies of
*A FAITH THAT IS REAL*
and other Victor titles
wherever good books are sold.

If you have enjoyed this book,
or if it has had an impact on your life,
we would like to hear from you.

Please contact us at:

VICTOR BOOKS
Cook Communications Ministries, Dept. 201
4050 Lee Vance View
Colorado Springs, CO 80918

Or visit our Web site:
www.cookministries.com

*Victor*®
The Bible Teacher's Teacher